Pray with Me

"*Pray with Me*, a practical, down-to-earth guide, is filled with suggestions for helping you, your children, and your grandchildren to make prayer a part of everyday life. The author examines memorized prayer, sung prayer, lectio divina, Ignatian and other forms of prayer, and how to experience them with youngsters. At the same time, it assists parents and grandparents in deepening their own prayer life, leading to strong family bonds with Jesus and one another."

Cardinal Timothy M. Dolan
Archbishop of New York

"In *Pray with Me*, Grace Mazza Urbanski walks alongside parents in a thoughtful consideration of the gift of prayer. Grace shares from her theological expertise and a mother's caring heart to inspire you into a dialogue with God and your family. She gives us highly useful ideas to make prayer an active part of our domestic church. I highly recommend this for any parent, grandparent, son, or daughter looking to grow closer to God and their loved ones."

Lisa M. Hendey
Founder of *CatholicMom.com* and author of *The Grace of Yes*

"Grace Mazza Urbanski has gifted us with a smart, engaging, and thoughtful book to jump-start prayer life with our children. *Pray with Me* is a great way to invite young parents to see the goodness of God in the midst of the messy calling known as parenting."

Tim and Sue Muldoon
Authors of *Six Sacred Rules for Families*

"At the turn of millennium, Pope St. John Paul II said that our communities need to be 'schools of prayer.' Through personal stories and very practical suggestions, Grace Mazza Urbanski provides the material for families to become schools of prayer. She does so in a humorous and moving way that makes *Pray with Me* both fun and inspiring."

Rev. James Kubicki
National director of the Apostleship of Prayer

Pray with Me

Seven Simple Ways to Pray with Your Children

Grace Mazza Urbanski

AVE MARIA PRESS AVE Notre Dame, Indiana

Founded in 1865, Ave Maria Press is a ministry of the United States Province of Holy Cross.

www.avemariapress.com

Paperback: ISBN-13 978-1-59471-574-7

E-book: ISBN-13 978-1-59471-575-4

Cover image © Katherine J. Ross.

Cover and text design by Katherine J. Ross.

Printed and bound in the United States of America.

Library of Congress Cataloging-in-Publication Data
Mazza Urbanski, Grace.
  Pray with me : seven simple ways to pray with your children / Grace Mazza Urbanski.
    pages cm
  Includes bibliographical references.
  ISBN 978-1-59471-574-7 -- ISBN 1-59471-574-2
  1. Prayer--Christianity. 2. Christian education of children. I. Title.
  BV215.M3725 2015
  248.3'2085--dc23
                            2015014520

Contents

Introduction

One of my earliest memories as a child comes from a bitter Wisconsin winter night, the kind of night when you can hear the window frames shrinking from the cold. I was about six or seven years old, and my freezing toes woke me up in the middle of the night. I crept down the hall and across to my parents' bedroom. Sneaking up to my mom's side of the bed, I whispered,

"Mom, I'm really cold."

My poor mom, mother of eight children, rarely slept well. In fact, I doubt she'd gotten a full night's sleep in well over a decade. On this particular evening, she was in a deep sleep. I whispered more loudly,

"Mom. Mom! I'm really cold."

Mom stirred. "Hmm? Who?"

"It's me, Grace. I can't sleep because I am freezing."

In response to this, my mom spoke a complete sentence, leading me to conclude (mistakenly, it turns out) that she was conscious and coherent. What my mom said made perfect grammatical sense, but left me bewildered:

"Go get your Grace towel, spread it out, and lie down on it." (My "Grace towel" was my personalized bath towel depicting a cute ballerina.)

"What?"

"Your Grace towel. Spread it on the ground and lie down if you're cold."

Somewhat uncharacteristically, I obeyed. I tiptoed back down the chilly hallway and grabbed my towel. Returning to my parents' room, I spread the towel on the floor and lay down, colder now than ever.

I'm not certain how much time actually passed, but after what felt like three ice ages, my mom sat up, fully awake, and noticed me just as her foot threatened to step on my face.

"Grace! What are you doing?"

"I got my Grace towel like you told me to because I was cold."

My mom had no recollection of telling me any such thing, of course. Then it hit her: she had been dreaming. Gradually, my mom realized she'd been dreaming of a summer getaway at the pool. In her dream, I had just gotten out of the water, dripping and cold. She told me to lie down on my towel in the sunshine until I was warm and dry.

I tease my mom with this anecdote once in a while, joking she had not been dreaming but was actually using the Grace towel as a new form of punishment. Not long ago, this story popped into my head in a serious moment as I considered how to help my children pray. Essentially, the story depicts a child asking her parent for help. The parent offers what (imperfect) help she can, and eventually everything works out. This relates to prayer in two ways.

First, the story adds an amusing twist to Luke 11:9–13:

> And I tell you, ask and you will receive; seek and
> you will find; knock and the door will be opened to

you. For everyone who asks, receives; and the one who seeks, finds; and to the one who knocks, the door will be opened. What father among you would hand his son a snake when he asks for a fish? Or hand him a scorpion when he asks for an egg? If you then, who are wicked, know how to give good gifts to your children, how much more will the Father in heaven give the holy Spirit to those who ask him?

In a funny little way, my mom *did* pretty much hand me a snake when I had asked for a fish: the "snake" offered was an ice-cold floor, while the "fish" I longed for was an extra blanket or a few minutes of snuggling. Mom has a watertight alibi, of course: she was unconscious. When it comes to teaching children how to pray, many of us adults feel unconscious in our own way—unprepared, uncomfortable, unfamiliar, or indifferent. Nevertheless, when our children need help, we offer what we can. Ultimately, prayer is God's gift; he improves our imperfect attempts to help our children pray.

The second lesson this story highlights is that children listen more often than we give them credit for. I was as prone to disobedience as any child, even when asked to honor perfectly reasonable requests, yet I went to fetch the Grace towel. Why did I, for once, choose this particular moment to submit blindly to authority? For probably the only time in her life, my mom was talking nonsense, yet I obeyed. Mom offered me a scorpion, and I accepted it. Our children pay attention to us, even when we are not aware of it. Consciously or not, we always pass *something* on to our children. Let's give them prayer.

Jesus says, "Ask and you will receive; seek and you will find; knock and the door will be opened to you." Prayer involves asking, seeking, and knocking boldly on the very door of God's heart. Prayer is our active, personal relationship with God; it gives us access to God and permits God to reach into our lives and our hearts.

Children have a natural advantage in prayer. Jesus holds them up as models of faith: "'Amen, I say to you, whoever does not accept the kingdom of God like a child will not enter it.' Then he embraced [the children] and blessed them, placing his hands on them" (Mk 10:15–16). We must trust God, our heavenly Father, in all things, at all times. Accepting the kingdom "like a child" means acknowledging our dependence on our Father. Adults who care for children have the honor and the obligation to help them build on their natural openness to God by helping them cultivate life-giving prayer habits.

At times, prayer intimidates adults—parents, teachers, grandparents, foster parents, guardians, ministers. We think a prayerful person should also be a perfect person. I certainly wish I could be a better, holier person. I can be terribly selfish. Though I always want to deserve a "World's Best Mom" coffee mug, I probably don't. My phone tempts me when I should be cracking open a board game to play with my son. I yell about a messy room instead of using "kind words," as I expect of my children. If the baby cries, I sometimes pretend I'm deeply asleep, forcing my husband to take care of her. We all have examples of less than award-winning parenting moments, moments when we hand our children the proverbial scorpion.

Every once in a while, we get it right, though, don't we? Maybe we even get it right more often than we realize. Jesus says we do. He affirms our instinct to "give good gifts" to our children. Asleep or awake, we sometimes burden our children with our mistakes. Perhaps we can all think of disadvantages or dysfunctions we received from our parents. There is no doubt we sometimes hand them down to our own children. However, Jesus invites us to focus on the beautiful hope he plants deep in our hearts, our fundamental desire for our children's good. That's an excellent definition of love, after all: to will the good for another. When we look at the "Grace towel" story another way, we recognize that my mom desired the good for me *even in her sleep*. That's what I call love.

We know that children can disobey, disrespect, and take for granted the adults who care for them. Regardless of their attitude toward adults, however, children depend on us. Children can't give birth to themselves, feed themselves, or protect themselves. God invites and equips adults to provide for children's basic survival as well as for the development of their natural aptitude for trusting God— for being in relationship with him. We get to show our children the world of prayer. We get to help them nurture their trust in God. We don't trust what we don't know, of course, which is why prayer comes in handy. Prayer helps us know God and develop our relationship with him.

Let's pray right this minute. Scripture is a privileged place to encounter Jesus, so let's return in prayer to that passage in Mark, "Then he embraced [the children] and blessed them, placing his hands on them."

How do you react when you read those words? Can you imagine Jesus embracing you, blessing you, placing his hands on you? What is that like? What is Jesus like? Are his hands rough? Smooth? Look at Jesus. He is gazing at you. How does it feel to look into the eyes of Jesus? Remain in that gaze for a moment. Soak it in.

Stay there.

A little longer.

Amen.

That was prayer. That was a personal encounter with Jesus prompted by scripture and guided by the Holy Spirit. It's just one moment in the trillions of moments that make up your relationship with God. Maybe this prayer was painful, if it stirred a memory of other hands, hands that did not touch gently. It's possible this prayer was shocking or unfamiliar, which either intrigued you or left you skeptical. I hope this prayer comforted you, amused you, or made you smile. Maybe you breathed a little more deeply as you rested in Jesus' embrace.

So many different kinds of prayer exist, so many different ways to encounter God. This book explores seven different kinds of prayer. (The kind of imaginative prayer we just experienced appears in chapter 3.) Seven kinds of prayer, out of a bazillion prayer possibilities. This book is not exhaustive; it's a start. It's also a jump-start for adults who already pray with the children in their lives but who don't mind a little encouragement or a few new ideas.

I am a wife and a mother of five children, though for a while I seriously considered the call to religious life. I'm a writer, a reader, a singer, and a wickedly good computer-game player. I have degrees in English and Theology.

Like St. John Paul II, I am a phenomenologist. I dearly love the leisurely study of abstract ideas, but I always need a concrete reference point to test those ideas. How I experience things and what things mean in my daily life provide rich soil for reflecting on who I am and what it means to be human. When it comes to prayer, I'm similarly practical. I want to know what prayer is and how it affects my daily life. By diving in and trying various forms of prayer, I come to know the meaning of prayer. The desire to know my Creator flows from my inner life, and I want to experience what it's like to live as a created being. I didn't create myself, and I won't die alone. I have a personal, loving God who is interested in every last detail of every day I live. Prayer helps me pay attention to the truth of my place in God's world.

What does prayer mean to you? How does praying affect your daily life? These are good questions to keep in mind as we move through this book together, exploring various ways to nurture our children's personal prayer.

I pray that this book becomes a helpful tool for all of us parents, all of us adults who care for children. I pray that God guides us and our children to frequent and fruitful prayer. St. Paul counseled the Thessalonians to "pray without ceasing" (1 Thes 5:17). I pray that this book makes St. Paul's words seem not ridiculously impossible but inviting, even exciting. I pray for people who wouldn't go near a book on prayer. I pray for people who don't have children or who have lost children, especially those who grieve. As Director of Children's Ministry at the Apostleship of Prayer, I pray energetically for all of God's children, and I pray for you. As Pope Francis says so often, please pray for me.

CHAPTER 1

Praying Spontaneously

Now, therefore, my eyes shall
be open and my ears attentive
to the prayer of this place.
—**2 Chronicles 7:15**

With all prayer and supplica-
tion, pray at every opportunity
in the Spirit.
—**Ephesians 6:18**

The Gospel of John shares this beautiful prayer of Jesus: "Father, I thank you for hearing me. I know that you always hear me; but because of the crowd here I have said this, that they may believe that you sent me" (Jn 11:41–42). Raising his eyes to heaven and praying these words, Jesus is not following a formula. He is not referring to a book of prayers. He simply describes what he is doing and how he is feeling. Without prior preparation, he asks from his heart for what he wants. This is spontaneous prayer.

Romano Guardini, an Italian-born priest who was raised and educated in Germany, believes spontaneous prayer is the "prime language of prayer." He writes, "The most vital prayer is the one which springs unprompted from the heart."[1]

Whenever we share with God what's on our heart, we are praying spontaneously.

Shaking his head sadly, a close friend once told my children, "Your mother has no filter." It's true. I often say just exactly what pops into my head. When I was teaching English at a Catholic university, my students compiled a booklet of all the spontaneous things that gushed out of my mouth during class. It was a long booklet. For some reason, the Quaker Oats man figured prominently in my analogies and examples that semester. Thankfully, I've been learning how to filter myself more successfully, but I have also been working on "baptizing" the impulse to share what's on my heart. Instead of censoring myself entirely (which would probably be impossible anyway), I try to accept my spontaneous thoughts and feelings and offer them to the Lord. When I blurt out something like, "Why is the Internet connection so slow?" I can address that question not to the universe at large but to a person: Jesus Christ. In so doing, I keep a comfortable conversation going between God and myself throughout the day.

We are individuals and adults who care for children. The more comfortable we are with keeping up a conversation with God each day, the more our children will see how God touches every aspect of our lives. Like an enthusiastic best friend, God loves to hear from us about even the most mundane details of our lives. God wants to share our prayers, thoughts, words, actions, joys, sufferings, and temptations. Jesus affirms this when he picks out the single greatest commandment of the whole law: "You shall love the Lord, your God, with all your heart, with all your soul, and with all your mind" (Mt 22:37).

Nothing is omitted. Spontaneous prayer invites God into the fullness of each day. Children enjoy considering how God cares about what books they read, what games they play outside, which jammies they wear to bed, and what they think about others in their heart.

Spontaneous prayer helps us remember to include the Father, Son, and Holy Spirit in our everyday lives. Sometimes it is helpful to choose certain predictable actions to trigger brief conversations with God: hitting *send* on e-mails, washing dishes, buckling a seat belt, putting on shoes, facing a recurring temptation, looking in the mirror. All of these moments can remind us we are in relationship with God and, therefore, lead to prayer.

Prayer Triggers

One of the most practical ways to help children develop the instinct to pray is simply to pray in their presence, speaking out loud about God and to God at any given moment of the day. Lots of families I know model spontaneous prayer to their children when they hear the siren of an emergency vehicle. No matter what they're doing at the time, they stop and say a quick prayer for the people who need help and for the personnel responding to the emergency. The siren acts as a prayer trigger. What are some other prayer triggers? Take a minute now and think of one or two prayer triggers for you, things that tend to make you sigh or cry out, whether in joy, grief, boredom, or frustration. How would your day be different if you caught a glimpse of God in those moments?

St. Peter Faber, one of the earliest companions of St. Ignatius in the Society of Jesus, loved to encounter God in spontaneous prayer. For him, almost anything could serve as a prayer trigger. On St. Peter Faber's canonization day, December 17, 2013, Fr. Adolfo Nicolás, S.J., said this about the new saint: "For Faber, any circumstance, place, or moment was an occasion for an encounter with God."[2]

No matter what our state in life, our days are comprised of circumstances, places, and moments—all opportunities to encounter God. St. John Chrysostom gave a homily on prayer that compared spontaneous prayer throughout the day to seasoning a dish: "Our soul should be directed in God, not merely when we suddenly think of prayer, but even when we are concerned with something else. If we are looking after the poor, if we are busy in some other way, or if we are doing any type of good work, we should season our actions with the desire and the remembrance of God. Through this salt of the love of God we can all become a sweet dish for the Lord."

Think of how many times a day we are "busy in some other way," as St. John Chrysostom put it. Parents, teachers, and other adults caring for children constantly attending to children's needs. When those immediate needs are met, we continue to interact with our children, talking, laughing, crying, playing, singing, studying, and learning together. All of these moments are opportunities for prayer. Let's let our children hear us offer heartfelt words to God! We can model spontaneous prayer for children by telling God what we're doing or feeling in our own simple words, encouraging children to do the same.

- Praise: "God is great!" "What a beautiful snowfall! Praise God!"
- Petition: "Please help my ear infection." "I'm sorry for yelling at my brother—forgive me." "I feel upset, Jesus; help me."
- Intercession: "Please help Grandma in the hospital." "Be with the children who go to bed hungry, Lord."
- Thanksgiving: "Thank you for my family!" "Thank you, God, for letting my friend come over."

Prayer is not complicated. It doesn't require a lot of time or energy. It is just talking and listening to someone we know, "a close sharing between friends," as St. Teresa of Avila liked to say. Prayer is completely natural, in the sense that God plants within us and our children a desire for God. We cultivate our relationship with God just as we do our other relationships, except for this: the Other in this Creator-creature relationship is perfect and eternally generous. What a relief! God will never make a mistake in his relationship with us. We can trust him completely. There is no need to feel bashful; we can simply start talking to God.

St. Thérèse wrote in her autobiography, *Story of a Soul*, "For me, prayer is a surge of the heart; it is a simple look turned towards heaven; it is a cry of recognition and love; embracing both trial and joy." To me, this quotation shows the power of developing the habit of spontaneous prayer. Cultivating an instinct to turn to God any old time—but especially at peak moments—confirms that we are truly children of God. Out of love God brought us into existence, and out of love God provides for us at all times. Children who learn this will approach both joy and suffering with confidence.

"One Cannot Give What One Does Not Have" (Maybe)

Popular wisdom tells us we can't give to others what we don't have ourselves. This implies that adults must have robust prayer lives of their own if they wish to help children learn how to pray. I disagree. I have passed on to my children a variety of things I myself don't have. Throughout their grade school years, for instance, my children thought I was simply crazy about math. We tackled all sorts of math and counting games; we gushed about how fun mental math is; we raced to see who could solve the most multiplication and division facts. It was an absurd charade. I do love analytical puzzles and patterns and several other mathematical concepts, but for the most part numbers bore me. I had wanted each child to embrace math, to thrill to the challenges math hurls in their paths, and never to destroy their growing mathematical abilities by muttering the uncreative phrase, "I hate math."

I threw myself into an aggressive family effort to embrace math. And it worked. Math isn't necessarily the favorite subject of each of my children, but our pro-math attitude prevents the children from giving up and encourages them to consider the beauty of God's logic in the universe.

In a similar way, adults who care for children don't necessarily have to have a remarkable commitment to personal prayer to help children discover the practice—*but it certainly helps.* My relationship with math facts is totally unlike my relationship with the living God who created me out of nothing and lovingly keeps me alive. If I were numerically illiterate, life would be difficult and bewildering; but life without God is simply impossible. As St. Paul quoted to the Athenian pagans the words of their own poet, "In him we live and move and have our being" (Acts 17:28). Even if we adults don't have the world's most active prayer life, we somehow know St. Paul is right. Deep in our hearts, we know God is the reason "we live and move and have our being." That's why we have an instinct to lead our children to prayer.

Leading little ones to Jesus will not leave us unaffected. When we encourage children to pray, we might very well see for ourselves the natural attractiveness of prayer. How do we feel, after all, when we are in the presence of someone who loves our children? Don't we instinctively draw nearer to that person?

When one of my daughters was experiencing anxiety issues in grade school, I worried that her teacher and classmates would begrudge the effort required to accommodate her extra needs. I sat at home during the school day and fretted about whether the teacher would lose patience if my daughter burst into tears because, for example, the daily schedule had been changed without warning.

I approached our first parent-teacher conference with some trepidation. When the evening arrived for us to sit down with the teacher, she began the meeting by looking us in the eye, smiling, and saying in all sincerity, "I love your daughter." I felt a heavy burden lift from me as I recognized in this teacher a fellow caregiver, a partner willing to love my child in any circumstance. It is no surprise that, a decade later, my heart melts every time I see this teacher.

Jesus loves our children this way, and perfectly, too. Adults who care for children will feel drawn to love the One who loves the children, who draws them close to his heart—the gentle shepherd who calls, "Let the little children come to me" (Mk 10:14). While we need not have disciplined prayer lives of our own to start leading children to prayer, we may soon find ourselves falling in love with the God of love as we accompany our children. Prayer is our living relationship with that love.

Children Deserve Our Best in Good Times and in Bad

When I speak to groups of parents, I often ask them what they want for their children. Phrased in various ways, the answer is basically the same: happiness. That means we want our children to get a good education, have lasting friendships, find success in sports or art or scholarship, fall in love, enjoy their careers, and, ultimately, live forever in heaven. Much of the work in ensuring this happiness involves looking toward the future. This is parenting: preparing our children for the future.

Yet our planning for their future happiness can feel overwhelming. A stay-at-home mom I know was so anxious that other people's children might develop faster than her daughter that she enrolled her perfectly content one-year-old in day care so she could be "socialized": "I don't want her to get behind or feel socially obsolete because she has been at home full time." Now this may have been just what that particular toddler needed, but my heart ached for this mom. She had convinced herself that, although she was keeping her baby healthy and happy in a cozy home environment, she was not adequately equipping the baby for college.

Planning for—and praying about—college is a good thing. If, however, we focus so much on the future that we forget to pay attention to the moments of each day, we miss opportunities for prayer and opportunities to develop our children's relationship with God, who is the source of all success and happiness. Parents are the first and best teachers of their children. Meeting the needs of tomorrow starts by digging deep into today: staying close to our children and modeling spontaneous prayer to help establish in them the habit of paying attention to their friendship with God.

Schoolteachers, catechists, grandparents, and other adults play a vital role in helping children cultivate their friendship with God. Where would we be without them?

Even so, every schoolteacher knows that learning the language of God requires reinforcement in the home. Parents are the first gift God gives children. Blessed Adolph Kolping, a nineteenth-century German priest, once said, "The first thing that a person finds in life and the last to which he holds out his hand, and the most precious that he possesses, even if he does not realize it, is family life." The family is the first place children learn love. Praying spontaneously throughout the day is a tool mothers and fathers give to their children to help them love the God who made us all.

While we can encounter God in any old circumstance of the day, sometimes suffering is the thing that gets our attention. God cannot will evil, but when suffering occurs, we know he accompanies us in an intimate way.

When my son Paul was in the fourth grade, he was the victim of bullies. Paul's tormentors decided he was stinky and contagious. It began as just an obnoxious joke with one or two boys, but then the girls got in on the game. By the time I learned about the situation, Paul's "disease" was an established fact in the fourth grade.

For months, no classmate would stand next to Paul in line or sit next to him on the bus for fear of being infected. Apparently Paul endured this in silence. He never said a word about it to my husband or me. We might never have known had the taunting not escalated. The girls decided to start leaving dirty things in Paul's backpack. A rotten banana, squished into every crevice of his bag, was my introduction to Paul's situation.

When Paul came home from school and started to unpack his backpack, I noticed that thick banana goo coated *everything*. I helped him pick out his slimy belongings, one by one. When we got to the six-hundred-page Harry Potter book (borrowed from a friend), I wanted to scream. The book was ruined. I asked Paul for an explanation, and his whole heartbreaking story came pouring out. I went to my bedroom, closed the door, and called the mom of the child Paul identified as the ringleader. After a brief (and miraculously calm) conversation, she hung up on me.

My heart raced as I held the disconnected phone in my hand. All my anger and hurt for my son, as well as bad memories of my own childhood miseries, assaulted me. First, I wanted to call my brothers (I have six) and let them know about Paul's bullies. Since I am 50 percent Italian and 50 percent Irish, I wanted to call in some family protection in retaliation. Next, the desire to hold this grudge in my heart till the day I died flared up in me. In the midst of my vengeful fantasizing, it suddenly occurred to me to pray. But I couldn't think of any words. I calmed myself down and went to find Paul.

"Paul, I tried to talk to that mom to see if we could find a way to make things better for everyone at school, but the phone call didn't go well. I am feeling really upset, and I don't know what to do next. Can we please pray together?"

"Sure, Mom. I'll start."

Although I don't remember Paul's exact words, I distinctly remember feeling lifted up and carried in God's loving arms as Paul prayed aloud. I remember he started our spontaneous prayer with what I would have described as a penitential rite: he acknowledged that everyone makes bad choices at times and that he was sorry for ever being a bad friend to anyone at school. My ten-year-old boy went on to pray for the students at school, for their parents, and for himself, that God would make him strong and cheerful. I might have been the one to suggest we pray together, but my child was the one who taught me how to pray in that moment.

Spontaneous prayer allowed me to pay attention to something other than my grizzly-bear-momma rage in that moment. Taking turns praying with my son showed me what he was thinking and feeling. We invited God into the situation and asked the Creator of the universe to help us with a mess that felt out of our control. Praying reminded me that the Father had not abandoned my son, just as he never abandoned Jesus in his Passion and death. Spontaneously placing our difficulties in the hands of the Father did not clean up the banana goo in the backpack, but it changed my heart. Frantic anger was replaced with the quiet confidence of the Resurrection.

After we prayed, Paul and I decided we would talk to his teacher and the principal. This should have been my first instinct, but somehow I had thought it was better for the parents to try to work things out with the children. Naturally, our school had policies in place to work through the challenges, and our principal, a wise and gracious woman, invited Paul to be part of the conflict resolution. In a remarkably short time, the mob mentality subsided. Paul is now in high school, and he has strong friendships with many of the classmates he once faced as adversaries. Only the power of God can accomplish that kind of genuine reconciliation. Prayer increases our access to this power.

I know that inviting Jesus into our difficulties allowed his grace to flow into the situation, into our hearts and the hearts of others. Many families I know have endured truly excruciating events: the death of a child or spouse, divorce, mental illness, infertility, an adult child's rejection of faith, and more. These families inspire me. They have testified that prayer makes things better. Spontaneous prayer makes good times even sweeter by connecting our momentary happiness to the eternal joy of God. Spontaneous prayer makes bad times sweeter, too, by opening our hearts to the power of God. Challenges that seem unbearable become possible to endure.

Touching God

Acquiring the habit of spontaneous prayer helps our children recognize God in the situations and persons we encounter throughout the day. The more natural this habit becomes, the stranger it is to exclude God from our daily encounters. We all know what it feels like to receive a jolt when we suddenly realize we are missing something that is always there—if a wedding ring is suddenly not on its finger or the Statue of Liberty disappears. How powerful it would be to grow so prayerful, so accustomed to the presence of God, that we become alarmed during the day when we realize we have stopped touching God.

When I became pregnant with my fifth baby, our oldest child had just turned seven. I was exhausted. I hunted sleep like a starving hyena scans a herd for pitiful stragglers at the fringes. Usually not an enthusiastic fan of screen time for children, I grew to love the thirty-minute splendor of *Blue's Clues* and *VeggieTales*. My preschoolers learned about video marathons. I learned how to protect the couch cushions from my drool.

One morning, I popped in a show. Feeling sleep overpowering me, I lay down on my side and arranged the children atop me so I could be sure they didn't wander off. I called this phenomenon the "Mommy Mountain." In a little while, my barely conscious brain detected a void on "Mommy Mountain." I opened one eye to confirm that Jack, then two years old, was no longer in the room. I propped myself up and asked four-year-old Ann for a favor, "Ann, could you please go see where Jack is? You don't have tobother him, you don't have to talk to him; just please find him and then run right back to me and tell me what he's doing."

In a few seconds, Ann returned with this report: "Jack is in your bedroom. He's drinking beer."

I dashed upstairs to find Jack lowering the beer bottle from his lips and wiping his mouth with his sleeve. My husband had opened a beer the night before and had left the bottle on his nightstand. I gathered up Jack and immediately wrote an e-mail to my husband at work: *If you can remember how much beer you left in the bottle last night, I can calculate how drunk our son is right now.*

As it turns out, it had been mostly just foam remaining in the bottle, so Social Services was never notified. After all that excitement, I began to prepare lunch, carrying

Jack on my hip. I opened the fridge, and Jack peered in, announcing, "We need more beer."

Strangely, that "Mommy Mountain" episode came to mind as I was reading Pope Francis's 2013 apostolic Exhortation *Evangelii Gaudium* (*The Joy of the Gospel*). The Holy Father writes, "I invite all Christians, everywhere, at this very moment, to a renewed personal encounter with Jesus Christ, or at least an openness to letting him encounter them; I ask all of you to do this unfailingly each day."[3]

It occurred to me that being open to a daily personal encounter with Jesus in spontaneous prayer is a little like the procedure I used (albeit with questionable success) to keep my children close and safe during pregnancy. In order to stay connected with my children, my most precious gifts on earth, I had to be creative. In my somewhat debilitated state, I had to seek new ways to make sure I was attentive to them. I was weak and tired, and I didn't trust my own power, so I connected myself, literally, to the bodies of my children. It wasn't a stellar example of mothering, but it was what I could manage.

Analogously, our relationship with God is the most precious gift we all receive from our Creator. The pope encourages us to seek new ways to connect ourselves, literally and figuratively, to the person of Jesus. Prayer allows us to pay attention to our relationship with God, especially when we feel weak and poor. We may not feel like stellar examples of faithfulness, but spontaneous prayer can renew our attempts—even feeble ones—to touch Jesus.

The more we pay attention to God by reaching out in spontaneous prayer and service, the more we may begin to notice the constant presence of God. If we try this "unfailingly each day," as the pope suggests, our mindfulness may become the norm. When Jack got up and left the "Mommy Mountain," his absence alarmed me, shook me out of my torpor. What a gift we give our children when we help them pay attention to God in spontaneous moments, a gift that will give them confidence in God and in themselves throughout life.

In the *Catechism of the Catholic Church* we are taught: "The acts of faith, hope, and charity enjoined by the first commandment are accomplished in prayer. Lifting up the mind toward God is an expression of our adoration of God: prayer of praise and thanksgiving, intercession and petition. Prayer is an indispensable condition for being able to obey God's commandments" (2098). In this quotation we see that the God who teaches us how to give is himself the best gift we can offer to our children. When we pray, we invite God into our home. Something miraculous happens: this God who is greater than all the galaxies settles cozily into the individual hearts of all the family members. The Incarnation astonishes us because the all-powerful God chose to become a human baby in the world; prayer astonishes us further as we discover how God chooses to dwell in our own hearts. One young mother I know, a good friend of mine, is constantly humbled and surprised to realize that God already has a personal relationship with each of her small children, a relationship she does not own or control. She feels keenly her mission to allow this relationship to grow.

Children are always already in relationship with God, so parents and teachers can help them cultivate daily prayer habits. Children amaze adults with their personal insights about God, insights not imposed by others but generated from their personal relationship with God.

A woman who called in to an interview I gave on Catholic radio shared an early memory: she vividly remembers lying on a changing table as a toddler, looking out of the window as her mother changed her diaper. She felt cared for, peaceful, and happy as she looked out at nature. She has always known that was a moment with God. When we invite the Blessed Trinity into our homes, schools, and daily lives, we encourage children to develop a vibrant religious imagination and to discover—and continually rediscover—a personal image of God that will develop as the child grows. This relationship belongs entirely to the child. It will, quite literally, save the life of the child because Jesus promised eternal life to those who know the Father.

In the Gospel of John, Jesus tells his disciples, "I will not leave you orphans; I will come to you. . . . On that day you will realize that I am in my Father and you are in me and I in you. . . . Whoever loves me will keep my word, and my Father will love him, and we will come to him and make our dwelling with him" (Jn 14:18, 20, 23). This scripture passage helps us see our goal as adults who care for children: we want God to come into their hearts (and ours) and make a home there. Prayer, which is our relationship with God, is the way we know God and open our hearts to him. This is what the apostle Paul confirms, in his own prayer for his spiritual children. With the apostle Paul, I close this chapter in prayer for you:

> For this reason I kneel before the Father, from whom
> every family in heaven and on earth is named, that

he may grant you in accord with the riches of his glory to be strengthened with power through his Spirit in the inner self, and that Christ may dwell in your hearts through faith; that you, rooted and grounded in love, may have strength to comprehend with all the holy ones what is the breadth and length and height and depth, and to know the love of Christ that surpasses knowledge, so that you may be filled with all the fullness of God. Now to him who is able to accomplish far more than all we ask or imagine, by the power at work within us, to him be glory in the church and in Christ Jesus to all generations, forever and ever. Amen. (Eph 3:14–21)

Chapter 1 Questions

~~~~~~

Exercise I: Personal Inventory for Parents and Teachers

Before introducing new prayer practices to their children, parents may find it helpful to reflect on their own prayer lives, their own relationships with God. Our relationships with other people can give us insights into our relationship with God, so these questions invite reflection on all kinds of relationships. Here are some questions to consider:

- What has been my most successful relationship with another person?
- Which personality traits of both the other and myself contribute to the success of that relationship?
- What kind of effort (pleasurable, routine, sacrificial, etc.) do I put into that relationship?
- Have any relationships in my life hurt me, causing me to lose trust?
- How has love changed my life?
- How do I respond to the idea that prayer is simply a relationship, relating with God?
- Deep down, how do I feel about putting more time and energy into my relationship with God?
- How do I pray now?
- What are my prayer triggers?
- How did I pray when I was young?
- What do I want for my child(ren) or students, ultimately?

Exercise II: Personal Inventory for Godparents

The primary task of godparents is to support parents in their efforts to nourish the faith lives of children. Here are some questions for godparents to consider:

- When did I meet my godchild?
- Why are his/her parents special to me?
- What is the date of my godchild's baptism? What did I accept as my role on that date?

- How do I try to stay involved with my godchild and his/her parents?
- How could I learn more about, and nourish, my godchild's relationship with God?

~~~~~~

Exercise III: Personal Inventory for Grandparents

An old Welsh proverb says "perfect love sometimes does not come until the first grandchild." More recently, Cardinal Timothy Dolan suggested that "grandmas and grandpas are among God's choicest gifts to us." Here are questions for grandparents to consider as they reflect on their unique role in the lives of their grandchildren:

- How do I pray now?
- How has my prayer changed throughout the stages of my life?
- Do I talk about prayer with joy and openness?
- Do my grandchildren and their parents know I am interested in all the aspects of their lives (emotional, educational, physical, and spiritual)?
- How could I learn more about, and nourish, my grandchildren's relationship with God?

CHAPTER 2

Praying from Memory

Take to heart these words
which I command you today.
Keep repeating them to your
children. Recite them when you
are at home and when you are
away, when you lie down and
when you get up.
—**Deuteronomy 6:6–7**

This is how you are to pray:
Our Father in heaven, hallowed
be your name. . . .
—**Matthew 6:9**

When I was in kindergarten, Congress created the pres-
ent-day Department of Education, launching America into
a storm of education reforms. The current Common Core
debate reminds us that these education reforms often cause
controversy. Memorization has generated debate for years,
as education experts alternately vilify and champion the

practice of requiring students to memorize material. Many colorful, animated memory apps have recently appeared on the market, however, suggesting that rote memorization may be coming back into favor.

To Memorize, or Not to Memorize, in the Google Age

Personally, I have always been a fan of memorization, despite (or perhaps because of) not being gifted with a particularly robust memory. In the Google Age, facts are always just a click away, but I often become annoyed with myself when I am forced to do an Internet search for something I should just . . . *know*. When Afghanistan and other Middle Eastern countries jumped into the news after 9/11, I was ashamed that I'd never memorized the geography of that region. When the United States invaded Iraq, I had no mental context for the battle and had to spend time searching for maps of the Middle East. Although the maps I needed were just a click away, I was frustrated and embarrassed that I didn't know the region. Memorization would have provided immediate access to helpful details even if I was nowhere near a computer.

Not everyone is enthusiastic about memorization. Jean-Jacques Rousseau in the eighteenth century and John Dewey in the nineteenth and twentieth centuries were both prominent educational philosophers who saw memorization as a threat to spontaneity. More recently, in a 2013

Atlantic article, educator Ben Orlin decried memorization tactics, stating, "They don't solve the underlying problem: They still bypass real conceptual learning. Memorizing a list of prepositions isn't half as useful as knowing what role a preposition plays in the language." Orlin goes on to explain: "What separates memorization from learning is a sense of meaning. When you memorize a fact, it's arbitrary, interchangeable—it makes no difference to you whether sine of $\pi/2$ is one, zero, or a million. But when you *learn* a fact, it's bound to others by a web of logic. It could be no other way." Well, of course, learning—not empty reciting—is a thinking person's ultimate goal. But, as Orlin himself admits, "A head full of facts—even memorized facts—is better than an empty one."[1]

As the *Catechism* states, "The memorization of basic prayers offers an essential support to the life of prayer, but it is important to help learners savor their meaning." (2688)

Romano Guardini, one of the most important religious thinkers of the twentieth century, believed that "the spirit soon wearies of empty reciting." When discussing how to recite the Rosary, the mother of all memorized prayer, Guardini cautions against praying by rote: "To recite the Rosary in a hurry is not only wrong but absolutely pointless: it must be spoken slowly and thoughtfully. If there is no time for the whole Rosary one should do one section only; it is better to recite a part in the correct manner than the whole of it with insufficient care."[2]

If we guard against "empty reciting," memorized prayer provides an encounter with God. The Bible itself shows examples of memorized prayer, recited over and over again—even eternally.

- **Psalm 55:17–18:** The Old Testament refers often to the Jewish practice of praying prescribed prayers three times a day. "But I will call upon God, and the LORD will save me. At dusk, dawn, and noon I will grieve and complain, and my prayer will be heard."
- **Matthew 26:44:** In the garden of Gethsemani, Jesus goes off a little way from his friends to pray, using formulaic words. "He left them and withdrew again and prayed a third time, saying the same thing again."
- **Revelation 4:8:** The angels and elders repeat prayers forever. "The four living creatures, each of them with six wings, were covered with eyes inside and out. Day and night they do not stop exclaiming: 'Holy, holy, holy is the Lord God almighty, who was, and who is, and who is to come.'"

Learning By Heart

Memorized prayer can become robotic, but consider another phrase we use to describe memorization: *learning by heart*. Prayers learned by heart nourish us. Sometimes these recited offerings come to us when our own words fail. What's more, they connect us to our massive faith community. Over the centuries and across the globe, Jesus and his followers have written prayers we receive and pass on as part of our heritage of faith.

Memorized prayer might also work miracles in a critical moment. Contemporary Catholic speaker Rosario Rodriguez instinctively turned to prayer when a man tried to assault her. Although his hand covered her mouth, she screamed the Hail Mary as loudly as possible. Inexplicably, he suddenly let go of her and ran away.[3]

Immaculée Ilibagiza, famed survivor of the Rwandan genocide, writes powerfully about memorized prayer in her autobiography *Left to Tell*. For weeks, she and seven other women avoided the tribal slaughter by huddling in a tiny bathroom hidden away in a neighbor's house. Eating little and speaking less, they crouched on the floor staring at each other for days and days. Ilibagiza outlived the inhumanity of it all by plunging deeply into prayer. The only personal item she had other than the clothes she wore was her father's rosary. She prayed those beads over and over, and in that memorized, formulaic prayer, she found her salvation.

> I found a place in the bathroom to call my own: a small corner of my heart. I retreated there as soon as I awoke, and stayed there until I slept. It was my sacred garden, where I spoke with God, meditated on His words, and nurtured my spiritual self. . . . I entered my special space through prayer; once inside, I prayed nonstop, using my rosary as an anchor to focus my thoughts and energies on God. The rosary beads helped me concentrate on the gospels and keep the words of God alive in my mind.

> I prayed in silence, but always mouthed the words
> to convince myself that I was really saying them . .
> . otherwise, doubt would creep in and the negative
> energy would come calling.[4]

Memorized prayers can, as Ilibagiza discovered, centralize
all our energies on the familiar words, liberating our minds
to imagine the gospel scenes and characters that inspired
the words of the prayer in the first place.

Freeing our imagination is really the goal of memorization. Memorizing prayers and scripture verses requires
fixing our full attention on a text. Think of how a kite is
assembled. We start with a solid framework, then fasten
the corners of the kite material onto it. The framework is
the prayer or scripture passage we wish to learn by heart.
Fastening the kite's material onto the framework represents
the mental effort required to latch on to the text. Once
the kite is thus assembled, we can launch it into the atmo-
sphere to fly free. In a similar way, once we have attached
our minds to the text we wish to memorize, we are free to
take those words with us without limitation.

In her book *Enriching Faith: Lessons and Activities on
the Bible*, educator and author Sr. Mary Kathleen Glavich,
S.N.D., encourages memorization for a rich spiritual life.
"When we memorize scripture verses," she writes, "they
can surface when we need them. We can repeat them as
prayers and quote them when we are trying to make a
point." Writing about scripture verses specifically, Sr. Glavich offers a variety of techniques to help children pray from
memory:

1. Reflect on the meaning of the verse. Visualize it. Look up unfamiliar words.
2. Repeat the verse aloud. Each time stress a different word.
3. Write the verse several times.
4. Display the verse where you will see it: on your desk, dresser, or refrigerator.
5. Make a jigsaw puzzle out of the words of the verse. Make two copies and race with a friend or family member in putting the puzzle together.
6. Make up motions to do as you say the verse.
7. Sing the verse to a tune.
8. If the verse is long, break it down and memorize one section at a time.
9. Work on memorizing a verse right before you go to bed. It sticks better.
10. Memorize verses while traveling, exercising, jogging, or waiting in the checkout line.
11. Set goals for yourself.
12. Be accountable to another person.[5]

Memory Is Character Itself

Memorization allows children to carry prayers with them everywhere and to free their imaginations to soar with texts learned by heart. Rote prayers have another, more relational benefit, too: they put the learner in close, prolonged, person-to-person contact with the author—a relationship.

When memorizing scripture or prayer, children encounter the Holy Spirit in personal relationship.

Anthony T. Kronman, Sterling Professor of Law at Yale Law School, believes in the relationship building that memorization provides to children. Kronman is an enthusiastic member of the pro-memorization camp: "Memorization has always been a useful method for acquiring knowledge," he writes in his book *Education's End: Why Our Colleges and Universities Have Given Up on the Meaning of Life*. According to Kronman's research, Harvard's founders appreciated memorization not only for its intellectual benefits but also for its personal blessings. "To acquire a text by memory is to fix in one's mind the image and example of the author and his subject. Memory is the storehouse of the soul. . . . We might even go so far as to say that memory is character itself; a man is what he remembers, and reveals himself to be the person he is in public speech."[6]

If we are open to Kronman's suggestion that "memory is character itself," then we see even more vividly the significance of Jesus' words: "In praying, do not babble like the pagans, who think that they will be heard because of their many words" (Mt 6:7). Memorizing scripture or prayer is a rich, personal encounter with the Holy Spirit. Babbling is not an option.

These strategies may help as we engage our children's hearts and minds through memorizing prayer:

• **Rhythm:** The rhythm of memorized prayer soothes children and babies—even babies in the womb! Expectant parents, try this: before your baby is born, say the same prayer every night before you settle into bed. Keep this up after the baby is born, and you'll notice the familiar prayer triggers relaxation and comfort.

- **Rhyme:** Rhymed prayer is easy to teach children. At first, toddlers will proudly fill in the end rhymes: "Angel of God, my guardian *dear*, to whom his love commits me *here* . . ." Before you know it, they'll have the whole prayer down.

- **Instinct:** Children who commit favorite prayers to memory have immediate access to them in any situation. The instinct to turn to memorized prayer brings stability and comfort at times when our own words may fail us.

- **Knowledge:** After the mechanical process of memorization is out of the way, children carry a whole text in their heads and in their hearts. They might not fully understand certain phrases at first—"thy kingdom come, thy will be done" is rather tricky—but they will grow in understanding as they mull over the familiar words, especially if we're praying with them!

- **Habit:** Praying from memory at routine times throughout the day creates a habit of talking to our loving God, of being in relationship with him. The Apostleship of Prayer especially encourages children to pray the morning offering. (See chapter 7 for more on praying the morning offering.)

When the disciples asked Jesus to teach them how to pray (see Matthew 6:9–13 and Luke 11:1–4), Jesus invokes rabbinic prayer formulas and gives them a prayer to memorize. Since that moment, countless Christians have stored the Lord's Prayer in their hearts. Let's help our children place themselves in our ancient tradition of praying from memory.

Our middle daughter, Ann, recently affirmed the wisdom of memorizing prayers. Like all of our children, Ann attends a private but nonreligious school. At the end of a particularly busy day in high school, Ann encountered one of her friends looking exhausted and distressed. Concerned, Ann asked her friend what was wrong. The short answer: a lot. This friend and her family were enduring sickness, death, and other hardships. Sadness and helplessness threatened to overwhelm both girls. In a moment of inspiration, Ann asked, "Would you like to pray?" The two friends slipped into a quiet stairwell nearby. Together, they prayed three memorized favorites: the Our Father, Hail Mary, and Glory Be. Exchanging a hug afterward, they proceeded on to their after-school activities, strengthened and consoled.

"Why those three prayers?" I asked Ann, and she couldn't say why. Maybe it was just a reflex. Maybe reciting familiar prayers was less awkward than inventing something profound on the spot. Maybe it was an act of hospitality, a welcome invitation to pray the same words in unison. Whatever the motivation, the girls' shared instinct to pray from memory connected them to each other and to their loving God, right there in the school stairwell.

Wherever we find ourselves during the day, with whatever joys, temptations, or burdens, memorized prayer can connect us, and our children, to God. "A Treasury of Memorized Prayers" appears at the end of the book in the appendix. My personal favorite memorized prayer is the one Jesus himself taught us.

Let's pray:

Our Father, who art in heaven,
hallowed be thy name;
thy kingdom come, thy will be done
on earth as it is in heaven.
Give us this day our daily bread;
and forgive us our trespasses,
as we forgive those who trespass against us;
and lead us not into temptation,
but deliver us from evil. Amen.

Chapter 2 Questions

1. Have you ever been asked to memorize something?
2. Have you ever learned something by heart, just for fun?
3. How does having something (a text, statistics, etc.) committed to memory make you feel?
4. How do you react when you hear someone reciting something learned by heart?
5. Are there things you wish you had memorized? What are they? And why would you like them instantly available by memory?
6. What would you like your children to know by heart?

CHAPTER 3

Praying with Scripture

Desire therefore my words;
long for them and you shall be
instructed.
—**Wisdom 6:11**

And Mary kept all these things,
reflecting on them in her heart.
—**Luke 2:19**

My husband (introvert though he is!) and I decided early in our marriage that our home would always be open to guests. We host family get-togethers, birthday parties, showers, music recitals, poetry slams, student dinners, prayer gatherings, farewell parties, small-group meetings, college reunions, movie nights, and holidays. We love inviting close friends and family, of course, but also people we've just met, travelers, and college students. Providentially, one of our daughters is a happy introvert; she encourages moderation in the coming and going, helping us to keep it all manageable.

Who are the people we invite into our homes or into our classrooms? Inviting someone over for an evening meal takes time and planning. Welcoming a guest speaker into a classroom requires consideration of lesson plans and, sometimes, administrative approval. Most of us think carefully about our guests, whom to invite and how to welcome them. All of the thought, preparation, and eagerness involved in offering human hospitality apply also to inviting God into our homes. This chapter focuses on inviting Jesus himself into our homes in a very real way by reading the Bible.

Reading scripture with the whole family welcomes Jesus into our homes. The Gospel of John opens with this startling sentence: "In the beginning was the Word, and the Word was with God, and the Word was God" (Jn 1:1). Jesus is that Word. As an English teacher, I am naturally delighted to see *the word* so elevated. I am enchanted by stories, language, and all manner of human communication. Words mean so much to all of us. No matter how they are signed or spoken, words symbolize what it means to be human.

Since the invention of the written word, we can hardly imagine history, philosophy, literature, or science without words. Even activities that seem purely numerical or physical—such as long division, dancing, playing a musical instrument, or fixing a car—would be difficult, even impossible, to learn without words. When the Gospel of John proclaims "the Word was God," we feel electrified: the actual *words* on the Bible page, inspired by the Holy Spirit, are the Word of God. That Word is the eternal Son of the Father, Jesus Christ. The words of scripture that we see and hear are a visitation of Jesus himself. In and through scripture, Jesus is present in our homes and our classrooms.

The thrill continues as we keep reading the first chapter of John: "The Word became flesh, and made his dwelling among us" (Jn 1:14). The Word (*logos* in Greek) is a lofty concept, but we can begin to understand the Word because he became a person. He pitched his tent with us and is still among us. He wants so much for us to pull up a log, grab the s'mores, and enjoy his company. Jesus wants us and our children to know the love that moved him to give his life for us. Every Christian adult I know who cares for children would feel proud to hear their children say, "I want to spend time with Jesus. I want to know him better." We all have an image of who Jesus is and what he said. What better way to deepen our encounter with that Jesus than to return frequently to the witness of his very words and actions? Reading scripture together is a privileged way to spend personal time with Jesus.

The Bible in Daily Life

Just One of the Books

Now I'm going to say something that might sound like a contradiction: don't set Jesus aside for special occasions! He is not wedding china. While we revere Jesus and acknowledge him as God, the King of kings, we humbly accept the earthiness of the Incarnation. Jesus chose to dwell among us, eating like us, wearing our fashions, walking to get places, working as a carpenter, and all the rest. This Jesus hasn't left us. He still wants to be with us in our everyday lives.

Children can feel as comfortable talking about Jesus as they do about the Very Hungry Caterpillar, a Wimpy Kid, Katniss Everdeen, or Captain America. We encourage this organic relationship with Jesus, the Word of God, when we make sure a children's bible or board books with Bible stories are among the books children grab every day. The Bible is unique, of course, since its author is God himself. Even so, children's bibles should feel just as familiar to them as any favorite storybook. If we want to cultivate natural prayer habits and mature faith lives in our children, we should integrate holy stuff into our normal routines, our daily lives.

Bible stories enrich the lives of even very young children. Yet sometimes we feel intimidated, hesitant about diving into scripture with our children. We moderns are efficiency experts, outsourcing every task we can to experts dedicated to various fields. We often streamline our lives by paying professionals to fix cars, install devices, press shirts, clean houses, care for preschoolers, and prepare meals. I can't even imagine what life would be like if I had to weave my own fabric or slaughter livestock for dinner. Yes, outsourcing has its benefits. We must not be tempted, however, to contract out our children's encounter with scripture. In 2010, Pope Benedict XVI's *Verbum Domini* encouraged parents to remember how important they are to children's relationship with scripture: "Part of authentic parenthood is to pass on and bear witness to the meaning of life in Christ: through their fidelity and the unity of family life, spouses are the first to proclaim God's word to their children."[1]

Pope Benedict understands that parents are the very first educators of their children. We parents can be prophets, proclaiming the Word of God in the intimacy of the home. The Lord said to Moses, "Take to heart these words which I command you today. Keep repeating them to your children. Recite them when you are at home and when you are away, when you lie down and when you get up" (Dt 6:6–7). Reading and praying with the Bible frequently— even every day—is a privilege, a bonding experience, and a sacred duty.

~~~~~~

Just Read It!

I recently attended a brilliant lecture on the Old Testament given by a university professor. He spoke with clarity and insight, filling everyone in the audience with the desire to know more about the scriptures. At the end of the talk, someone asked for book recommendations. The professor responded, "You want me to give you a list of books you can read to know the Bible better?"

"Yes, that's right."

"May I recommend . . . the Bible?"

Everyone chuckled, but he really meant it. "Dig into the Bible!" he insisted. "If you want to know more about the Bible and the people in it, simply pick up a bible and read."

Sometimes we may worry we won't know what a particular Bible story means or we won't be able to answer a child's question. Any anxiety that keeps us away from Jesus in the Word is not helpful. Jesus truly visits us in the Word; let's encourage our children to run into his arms. It's good for our children, in fact, for us not to know everything.

One of the best lessons children can learn is that knowledge requires effort. Imagine a child coming across this text in Matthew: "Do not think that I have come to bring peace upon the earth. I have come to bring not peace but the sword" (Mt 10:34). Parents or teachers might not immediately be able to explain just what Jesus means here. But a child will always benefit from hearing a respected adult say, "Those words seem different from other things Jesus says. I am not sure what Jesus means there, but let's find out together." And the adventure begins. Together the adult and child continue to read the passage, ask priests or lay ministers about the passage, bring it up in conversation with faithful friends, and, most importantly, consider Jesus' words in the intimacy of their hearts. This is praying with scripture.

Our family enjoys the tradition of reading from the gospel aloud at the dinner table. My husband and I always do the reading, unless it is a special birthday or feast day for one of the children; then it's a treat for the child to read to the family. Following the readings for each day's liturgy helps us feel connected to the universal Church, even if we

can't get to daily Mass. We read the gospel just before the
end of the meal, after the frenzy of passing dishes has subsided but before the food coma kicks in. After we read, we
ask each child an individualized, age-appropriate question
about the content, the details, the big picture, or the effect
the scripture had on him or her. A "correct" answer earns
dessert. And lo! We are merciful; we look more for loving
attentiveness than for precision. In the long history of our
dinner gospel readings, we can recall only one or two times
a spectacularly inattentive child really had to go without
dessert. Our oldest child recently made her Confirmation,
and we decided to amend the tradition: she no longer
receives a question about the gospel; instead, she offers her
own insight about what we heard.

Making the Word of God such a natural part of our
family routine has brought us closer to each other and to
the Lord. We frequently marvel at how the gospel of the
day, chosen years and years ago by people unrelated to us,
speaks prophetically to one or another of our family members. Often we have encountered something that day—a
prayer, work, joy, or suffering—that resonates in the words
of Jesus.

Our dinner conversations, which might have started
out with a series of fart jokes, have become incalculably
richer because Jesus is taking part. We read that Jesus tells
us to "turn the other cheek" (see Lk 6:29), and suddenly
a child will share how hurt she was at recess that morning
when a friend refused to let her play with the group. Jesus
invites Zacchaeus to come down from the tree, and we are
unexpectedly drawn into a conversation about how hard
it seems to find Jesus in the crowded world of school. It's

great to consider that Jesus is a nightly dinner guest at our house. He's so easy to cook for!

~~~~~~

Lectio Divina

Lectio divina (Latin for "divine reading") is a centuries-old prayer form experiencing a revival in formation programs. Many people have heard of lectio divina but aren't quite sure what it entails. It's simple and can fit nicely into a family's routine. Sunday afternoons work well for many families looking for ways to honor the Sabbath in a special way. Children as young as two can enjoy encountering Jesus in scripture through lectio divina. I recommend a bit of preparation before following the five steps, which I have adapted from *Verbum Domini*. A highly abbreviated, simplified approach for use with young children appears at the end of this section.

FAMILY LECTIO DIVINA IN FIVE STEPS

In preparation, choose a Bible story that is brief enough for the youngest child present to listen to attentively. Here are a few suggestions:

- Zacchaeus the tax collector climbing the tree (Lk 19:1–10)
- Jesus blessing the children (Mk 10:13–16)
- Jesus curing the bleeding woman (Lk 8:43–48)
- Jesus calling the first disciples (Mt 4:18–22)

Some families prefer to use the day's gospel reading from the lectionary, while others slowly work their way through a particular book of the Bible. Choose whatever scripture passage seems right for your family, but remember that scripture has the power to surprise. Sometimes an unlikely passage can provide a child with a profound encounter with Jesus.

Feel free to experiment with the lectio divina steps to find the process that works for your family. Each family's scripture time will look different—some families might choose to abbreviate certain steps while other families might skip over steps altogether at first, adopting the simplified lectio divina process added to the end of this section. God honors your desire to encounter him in scripture and will bless your time with him, whatever that looks like.

As you gather for time together with the Bible, consider lighting a candle or inviting everyone to bring a favorite blanket or stuffed animal. As reading scripture together in this way becomes a habit, muscle memory will kick in: each member of the family will associate physical relaxation and consolation with the Word of God. Invite everyone to sit comfortably, but attentively, neither slouching nor posing. Grow silent, perhaps by listening to the soft sounds of breathing. At first, a case or two of the giggles might erupt, but persevere. When everyone has settled into relative silence, begin the five steps:

Read *(Lectio)*

- Read the scripture passage aloud once. Then read it again.

- You may wish to appoint more than one reader, or even to read from two different versions of scripture (from a children's bible, for example, or from a different approved translation).

Meditate (*Meditatio*)

- Ask family members to identify silently a word, phrase, or image that especially stood out.
- Tell them to repeat that word or phrase silently or gaze at that image, in their minds and hearts. Turn it over and over like a jewel. Remind them that God wanted each of them to find this treasure today. If distracting thoughts or giggles interrupt, gently steer the focus back to the Lord. (See distractions as various parts of yourself rising to meet the Lord. If you find yourself thinking about what to make for dinner, for example, just acknowledge that your stomach gives praise to God, then gently set the dinner thoughts aside.)
- Allow this meditation time to last only as long as the youngest children can handle. Ten seconds might be a huge accomplishment! The more lectio divina becomes a habit of family prayer, the longer each person will enjoy the quiet reflection time.
- Now let all the family members share their thoughts aloud.

Pray (*Oratio*)

- Ask family members to speak silently to Jesus (or the Father or the Holy Spirit, if they wish).

- Remind them that prayer can take many forms.

  - Petition (prayers for yourself)
  - Intercession (prayers for others)
  - Thanksgiving
  - Praise
  - Blessing and adoration

- Let them know they can pray in words in the mind, in feelings from the heart, or in a simple, silent gaze at Jesus, who sees each one of us. Jesus loves us and knows us, our loves, our needs.

- These prayers can remain private, but some may wish to share their prayer with the rest of the family. Openness in sharing prayer is a great freedom and a gift; it can be encouraged but not forced.

Contemplate (*Contemplatio*)

- Now ask your family members to take a step further in their prayer by lingering with God, considering the ways he asks us to follow Jesus, to love him and others.

- Encourage everyone to ask, in silence, for the gift of seeing themselves as God sees them and for the wisdom to be the people God created them to be. Stay in this quiet contemplation period as long as the peace lasts.

- Now, aloud, close with a short prayer of thanks or praise. You might enjoy taking turns with the closing prayer, letting a different family member lead each

time. The prayer might be spontaneous words from
the heart or a family favorite, such as the Glory Be.

Act (*Actio*)

• Encourage family members to act on the insights
received in this time of prayer. Return to your daily
activities refreshed, strengthened, and ready to serve
the Lord by serving others.

SIMPLIFIED LECTIO DIVINA PROCESS

This is especially useful for families with young children.

1. Before bed, read aloud a short scripture passage.
2. Then read it aloud again.
3. Let each family member identify a word, phrase, or
   image that stood out and explain why.
4. Read the passage one last time.
5. After a few moments of silence, perhaps, close with a
   short prayer of thanks or praise.

Imaginative Prayer

St. Ignatius of Loyola, founder of the Jesuits, was an imagination maven. Through years of practice, reflection, trial
and error, prayer, and discernment, St. Ignatius developed
a heart-centered method for meditating on the scriptures

that has come to be known as Ignatian contemplation. It's similar to lectio divina in many ways, so practicing lectio divina with children is excellent preparation for introducing them to imaginative prayer.

Both lectio divina and Ignatian contemplation invite us to consider a particular scripture passage. In lectio divina, we hold on to a word, phrase, or image from the text and allow that to shape our personal interaction with God. In Ignatian contemplation, we use our imagination to insert ourselves into the Bible story. We use all of our senses to immerse ourselves in the moment.

Children in elementary grades through high school can enjoy the freedom of imaginative prayer. In 2008, Loyola Press published *Praying with Scripture*, a lovely little book of guided reflections for grade-school children. The booklet provides detailed scripts and step-by-step instructions for parents and teachers committed to formal sessions of meditation.

The prompts below follow the same tradition as that of *Praying with Scripture* but are more freely adapted to various age levels, including adults. St. Ignatius of Loyola knew the power of imaginative prayer, making it the bedrock of his classic *Spiritual Exercises*. Asking simple questions often unlocks the imagination; asking those questions in the context of prayer provides a personal encounter with Jesus Christ. Although St. Ignatius recommends spending an entire hour in contemplation, you might find it helpful to begin by praying for ten or fifteen minutes.

OPENING

- Sit comfortably, neither slouching nor rigid, and breathe deeply and gently.
- Make the Sign of the Cross and be aware of God's presence within, around, and beyond you.
- Imagine God looking at you with love.

PREPARATORY PRAYER

- Ask God that all you think, feel, and want may be for the greater glory of God.
- Let the Lord know that this prayer time is totally dedicated to him and to his desires for you.

SCRIPTURE

- Pick a Bible passage about Jesus and read it once to get a feel for it.
- What stirs your heart when you read it? Focus on that.

COMPOSITION

- Explore the place with your imagination, using all your senses.

- Imagine you are the person with whom Jesus is interacting. Where are you? Where is Jesus?
- Who is with you? How do they look? What are they saying? How do they sound?
- What else do you see? Hear? Taste? Smell? Touch?

GRACE

- Ask God for what you want from this specific time of prayer.
- Ask for grace to know Jesus more clearly, love him more dearly, and follow him more nearly.
- Ask for another grace if there is something else you desire from God. Ask from your heart.

CONTEMPLATION

- Read the passage again slowly, imagining you are part of it and that every word is for you.
- What feelings and thoughts arise in you?
- Pay attention to how you react to what is happening in contemplation.
- Let the Holy Spirit guide your prayer.

CONVERSATION

- Near the end of your time in prayer, imagine yourself alone with Jesus, gazing at one another.
- Talk to Jesus as one friend speaks to another.
- Tell Jesus what happened in this prayer—where you felt peaceful, scared, frustrated, happy, alive, or lonely. Share any worries, desires, or questions. Tell Jesus everything.
- Hear Jesus as he responds to you. How does he react? What is he saying to you through this scripture today? How does he feel about you?

CLOSING

- End your contemplation by praying the Our Father (or another favorite prayer) with feeling.
- Make the Sign of the Cross.

Getting the Children Involved

We have looked at three ways you can use scripture to pray with children:

1. casually surrounding yourself in Bible stories and simply diving in to scripture;
2. following the tradition of lectio divina; and

3.   learning how to encounter Jesus in the gospels through your imagination.

Let the children in your life choose. Young children will probably want to start with Bible stories. You can help them transition from stories to lectio divina. Later they can grow into longer moments of contemplation.

Praying with scripture welcomes Jesus into our homes and schools in a uniquely personal way. As St. John Paul II wrote in *Vita Consecrata*, "The Word of God is the first source of all Christian spirituality. It gives rise to a personal relationship with the living God and with His saving and sanctifying will."[2]

When we pray with scripture, we encounter the person of Jesus, the Word of God. When I visit schools, students routinely comment that our imaginative prayer exercise was their favorite part of our time together. Often, I ask students to imagine John 13:25, the moment during the Last Supper when the beloved disciple John leans his head against Jesus' chest. We spend several minutes imagining what we can hear, see, smell, taste, and feel leaning against Jesus. Many students approach me privately afterward or write notes to tell me they want to return there in prayer. They want to spend more time resting against the Heart of Jesus.

The children and youth I visit all around the country are naturally receptive to imaginative prayer. They honestly enjoy imagining themselves with Jesus in the context of the gospels, using their senses and imaginations as I lead them through questions like the ones in this chapter. Actually, after we're done with our five- or ten-minute imaginative

journey with Jesus, they're usually shocked when I suggest
we had been praying together. They thought prayer had
to feel dry and use only approved wording. Just spending
time with Jesus in the context of a scripture passage? Just
praying from the heart? It's a refreshing way to treasure
the Word ourselves and to pass on the gift of faith to our
children.

Think of the characters we met in stories when we
were young: Anne of Green Gables, Nate the Great, Christopher Robin, Fancy Nancy, Peter Pan, Cinderella, Tom
Sawyer. These and many other characters swim in our
imagination. We can describe them in detail: how they
look, what they do, what they say. We feel sure we would
recognize them if we met them on the street. Children can
likewise know the people revealed in the Bible: Abraham,
Sarah, Moses, Queen Esther, King David, Mary, Joseph,
Peter, James, John, Mary Magdalene, and, most of all,
Jesus himself. They can become part of the Communion
of Saints. The good news children will learn is that Jesus
Christ was a real man; his story is true. He lives, even now,
in heaven at the right hand of the Father and also with our
children and with us in our hearts.

Chapter 3 Questions

1.   Write down the titles of two or three of your most
     favorite books in the world.

- Do they have anything in common?
- Why do the particular words of these books strike you so powerfully?
- What are your feelings toward the books' authors?

2. How do you feel when you consider God, the author of creation?
3. Have you ever felt a Bible passage speaking directly to your circumstances, directly to your heart?
4. Have you ever spoken back to the author of the text in those moments?
5. How would your children's lives be different if they routinely encountered God in scripture?

CHAPTER 4

Praying with Song

Come, let us sing to the LORD,
and shout with joy to the rock
who saves us.
—**Psalm 95:1–2**

Be filled with the Spirit,
addressing one another [in]
psalms and hymns and spiritual
songs, singing and playing to
the Lord in your hearts.
—**Ephesians 5:18b–19**

Singing saturates prayer in love. In his commentary on the Psalms, St. Augustine writes, "He that sings praise, not only sings, but also loves him of whom he sings. In praise, there is the speaking forth of one confessing; in singing, the affection of one loving." St. Augustine connects singing with loving.

I am a singer, and I sing best when my heart is filled with love. Our family sings together every night before bed, which delights me. There are times, though, when I feel physical pain trying to make myself sing when I'm angry with someone or when prayer time arrives in the middle of an argument. Surely this is because singing integrates body and soul. If my mind is agitated, my body has a hard time singing a peaceful bedtime song. Making music requires the cooperation of the entire person. Lifting up the human voice in song, in prayer, involves reaching deep into the soul and exposing what lies there.

Research the Music

Though I know a few people who truly do not enjoy singing, researchers insist every culture in human history treasures music. All over the world, mothers sing lullabies to their babies, and grown-ups lift their voices to speak in a songlike voice to toddlers. Norman M. Weinberger, a psychology professor and founding member of the Center for the Neurobiology of Learning and Memory, writes that "Parents and caregivers instinctively communicate with infants in a musical fashion, because, although infants don't understand words, melodic stimulation always gets their attention. Young children clearly enjoy music, engaging in musical behavior spontaneously."[1] Weinberger has surveyed a wide range of studies that reveal the natural musical powers of children. He proposes that these musical abilities, demonstrated so early in human development, point to a biological predisposition of humans toward music. Humans yank out useless features, such as the appendix and wisdom teeth. We treasure music, though, and constantly create new songs, which suggests our bodies were designed for music. Humans need songs.

In *Why Music Moves Us*, psychologist Jeanette Bicknell, PhD, writes that "music can engage us deeply, taking us out of the world of our everyday care and concerns."[2] Citing previous research, Bicknell explains how music involves all the senses in "multi-sensory engagement," often stirring the imagination. We cannot be surprised that music triggers the imagination. Clearly we have reason to put more music, more singing, in our prayer time, especially with children who have enjoyed using imaginative prayer with scripture, as discussed in the previous chapter.

Dr. Daniel J. Levitin is a neuroscientist who runs the Laboratory for Musical Perception, Cognition, and Expertise at McGill University. Before entering the academic world, he was a professional musician, sound engineer, and record producer. Levitin studies what happens, neurologically, when we experience music, and also why humans have such an intense relationship with music. In his book *The World in Six Songs: How the Musical Brain Created Human Nature*, Levitin shows how we are actually biologically determined to incorporate music in human life.[3]

Levitin proposes that humans have always incorporated music into daily life, and he categorizes the music we make into six themes. I love when Levitin explains the relationship between communal singing and chemicals in the brain: singing together releases oxytocin, what Levitin calls a "trust-inducing hormone." Oxytocin is the same chemical released when a man and a woman create life together,

Levitin reminds us. Singing is *that* dramatic. When children make music together with the adults who care for them, we grow in trust, joy, appreciation, and attachment with each other—and with God.

Experience the Music

My own personal experience confirms this research. For most of my life, I have taken and given private voice lessons. When I teach voice, my first lesson with a new student is a trial—not like torture or the Final Judgment but a no-pressure stroll through my philosophy of working with the human voice. Students also can see if they like my approach and will be comfortable studying with me.

Some students are gregarious and eager, exploding into the music room ready to sing. Many other students, however, are desperately shy and fearful of singing alone in front of another person. I'm never surprised when someone gets a little teary at first. Singing is an intimate business. There's no external instrument to look at and manipulate, nothing to tune, polish, or string. There's just a body, the whole human body.

I remember meeting one high school student for her first lesson. Mary had been homeschooled her whole life and, although her close-knit family told her she had a lovely voice, she fretted about taking voice lessons. She spoke very little at our first meeting. She seemed unresponsive when I showed her the music theory books and vocal exercises I use.

I gradually got the feeling Mary was making up her mind not to return for a second lesson. Then, I asked her to sing. Her voice was bigger than I expected from such a quiet person, though tight and strained. Encouraged, I finished the lesson with a few words about how learning to sing is analogous to growing in the spiritual life: "When we train the voice, we're actually just getting out of its way. We spend a great deal of time focusing on the body at first, acquiring good habits of posture, breathing, and vowel production. Equipped with healthy habits, we progressively ignore the body, mindful of it only as the path the voice takes to run out from you toward others."

"That's spiritual?" Mary wondered.

"Sure!"

Encouraged, I ventured on.

"Many great believers have understood the secret to a holy life is to strengthen the body and mind, not for their own sake, but in order to put them at the service of others. You know, getting over yourself and letting God take control."

To my astonishment, Mary began to cry. She was also smiling and nodding. A deeply spiritual but tightly wound person, Mary loved the idea of freeing her voice, releasing it for the delight of others.

The voice is a direct gift from God. Like snowflakes, no two voices are exactly alike. But our God is the one who, as Gerard Manley Hopkins writes in his sonnet "Pied Beauty," creates the universe with breathtaking diversity:

GLORY be to God for dappled things—
　　For skies of couple-colour as a brinded cow;
　　　　For rose-moles all in stipple upon trout
　　　　that swim;
Fresh-firecoal chestnut-falls; finches' wings;
　　Landscape plotted and pieced—fold, fallow, and
　　plough;
　　　　And áll trádes, their gear and tackle and
　　　　trim.
All things counter, original, spare, strange;
　　Whatever is fickle, freckled (who knows how?)
　　　　With swift, slow; sweet, sour; adazzle,
　　　　dim;
He fathers-forth whose beauty is past change:
　　Praise him.[4]

"Pied Beauty" celebrates the diversity of creation. I often think of this poem as I consider how to approach the unique voices of my students; the fickle diversity of voices presents a challenge I love. Each voice sounds the way it does because of a unique assembly of physiology, genetics, experience, and personal history. What I tell my students in that first lesson is that my job is to help them find their purest, most powerful voice, first strengthening their anatomy to support that voice, and then showing them how to get their bodies out of its way.

St. Augustine claims singing is naturally bound up in loving, and another voice student of mine demonstrated that to me in a powerful way. Lucy studied with me throughout her high school years. A good all-around musician, Lucy had a nice alto sound. I saw her as a serious young woman and a hard worker. She learned a good number of songs from the standard alto repertoire and performed them well, though perhaps with less sophistication and color than we'd hoped for.

When Lucy returned home for summer after her first year away at college, she came back for a lesson. We chatted for a bit to catch up with one another, and I was thrilled to hear how enormously pleased she was with her school year. High school had been rather an affliction for Lucy, but her university was a perfect fit. Getting down to the business of singing, I played the opening arpeggio for Lucy to sing. The sound that came out of her mouth made me gasp and drop my hands from the keys. I exclaimed with delight, "Who *are* you?"

Lucy smiled but wasn't quite sure what had happened.

"You, Lucy, are a happy person. Your new college life suits you. Your singing tells me everything."

She'd only sung a few notes, but I immediately sensed her freedom. Her happier, more loving heart had given her voice a maturity and richness four years of vocal training never could. No matter how hard we work at something, such as singing or praying, love accomplishes more than we imagine.

Sing Everyday Prayers

Contemporary research finds singing helps make us more fully human. Biologically, singing releases chemicals in the

brain that make us happier, more hopeful, and more trusting. Spiritually, lifting our voices in sung prayer opens our
hearts as well. If we know children who want to grow
closer to God and to be more fully human, then it makes
sense to give singing a try. Like any activity that is a little
new, singing together gets easier when we do it every day.
Some families like to sing a favorite hymn every night
before bed. Incorporating hymns from church reinforces
the communal prayer that happens at church and helps
children feel more confident participating in the liturgy.
Our family rotates the hymns based on the liturgical season. My husband is a Latin teacher, so we like to throw a
little of that universal language into our seasonal singing.
Children learn quickly how to sing in other languages;
singing the prolonged vowel sounds helps get the new pho-
nemes in their ears. Thanks to the modern marvel of You-
Tube, recordings of these chants are only a click away.

Traditionally, these are the hymns or anthems the
Church sings during night prayer:

- *Alma Redemptoris Mater* (Holy Mother of Our
  Redeemer): sung from the first Sunday of Advent
  until the Feast of the Purification (February 2)
- *Ave Regina Caelorum* (Hail, Queen of Heaven): sung
  from after the Feast of the Purification until Easter
  Vigil
- *Regina Caeli* (Queen of Heaven): sung at the Easter
  Vigil through Pentecost
- *Salve Regina* (Hail, Holy Queen): sung from the day
  after Pentecost until Advent

These four anthems cover an entire year of night prayer, and they all ponder, through the eyes of Mary, the saving power of Jesus.

While singing the official anthems of the Church year appeals to some families and schools, others like to use already-familiar tunes in the children's native language. I regularly ask parents and teachers to share their favorite songs to sing with children. Here are some of the most popular songs, genres, and artists:

- "Jesus Loves Me" ("*Cristo Me Ama*")
- "Rise and Shine"
- "Amazing Grace"
- "This Is the Air I Breathe" by Rebecca St. James
- The Divine Mercy Chaplet in song, produced by Trish Short
- "10,000 Reasons" by Matt Redman
- "Holy Family" by Danielle Rose
- "This Little Light of Mine" by Harry Dixon Loes
- "I Want to Walk as a Child of the Light" by Kathleen Thomerson
- "My Soul Magnifies the Lord" by Chris Tomlin
- *Kids Sing for Jesus*, a CD by the Rennas
- *Share the Light*, a CD by Bernadette Farrell
- "Go Tell It on the Mountain"
- "Glory, Glory Hallelujah," the refrain from Julia Ward Howe's "Battle Hymn of the Republic"
- *Stories and Songs of Jesus* and *More Stories and Songs of Jesus*, CDs by Christopher Walker and Paule Freeburg, D.C.
- "The Baa, Baa Song" by Kevin Bueltmann

- "Lord, I Need You" by Matt Maher
- "Gather Together" and "God Loves Me" by John Burland
- The Litany of the Saints
- Vacation Bible School songs, especially ones with gestures
- Favorite hymns from church

In no way is this list comprehensive, or even very strategic. It's really just a collection of informal surveys and conversations. Happily, most songs are on YouTube, making them easy to access and learn.

Some parents use songs as audio cues with their children. One parent I met said she always sings Steve Angrisano's "Sacred Silence" when she feels herself growing frustrated with her children. "It calms me down," she shared, "and becomes a verbal cue that they need to cool it."

A couple of my own children love the excitement of overnight trips but get homesick as the night wears on. They find it helpful to take along and listen to a recording of our family's nightly prayers. Listening to the family singing helps them relax.

Singing songs as a family helps children and adults bond with each other and with God. If a parent or grandparent has to be away for a while, singing can make the separation easier. Many military families record the deployed parent singing a lullaby so children can listen every night to the familiar and beloved voice. Other parents, away for a few days on a business trip, call home and join in the nightly family song. The stability and trust singing together provides—even across miles—develops confident bonds of prayer.

Teachers know singing enhances any classroom environment. Sr. Bridget Smith, A.S.C.J., a veteran teacher of young children, says, "Singing is an essential part of any classroom but especially a religion lesson or any prayer experience." In a personal interview, I asked Sister to explain in more detail how singing and good pedagogy support one another.

> Singing with young children has many benefits in a classroom environment. It can serve as an aide to transition children from one activity to another: moving from another subject to a religion lesson or from one part of a religion lesson to another part. Some days, we walk around the room as we sing and the children repeat the gestures I do. A song can also be used to introduce or reinforce the objective of a lesson. Finally, because music can lift a child's mind and heart to God, singing can introduce and set the tone for a prayer experience, helping the children to focus and center themselves for the prayer.[5]

Singing enhances the learning and prayer of every child at home and in the classroom, including children with special needs. My now-deceased older brother Mark, born with severe mental and physical disabilities, including blindness, loved music. When his favorite albums were playing, he would move to the music, accompanying it with his unique vocalizations. Some children are less vocal than others, of course, or are sometimes entirely nonverbal.

Children with hearing challenges love to feel the rhythm of music pulsing through their bodies.

In Dr. Levitin's *The World in Six Songs*, he mentions laboratory tests he gave to people, asking them to match a certain beat. His research reveals people more successfully synchronize with one another than with nonhuman technology, such as a metronome. Most of us would expect it would be easier to match the digitally precise beat of a metronome, but no; people respond best with people. Humans making music together, even just a steady percussive beat, find synchronicity in one another. Music draws us together.

Music is a deeply human way to pray. Our bodies are equipped with a voice to sing and all kinds of body parts to make percussive sounds. Almost everyone can sing or make "a joyful noise" in one way or another. Singing with others releases healthy chemicals in our brains. And because singing requires the cooperation of all our body parts, we feel more integrated, more connected, when we sing. Music inspires wholeness and trust, and joining in song with others encourages attentiveness as we breathe together, begin together, and end together.

One of my best friends swears she is tone deaf, yet her entire family sings together every night "*Non Nobis, Domine*," the hymn made famous by Kenneth Branagh's film *Henry V*. Our family loves joining our voices to theirs when we get together for an evening. I never notice whether the notes or words come out right; I simply forget myself in the glorious experience of human friends all raising their voices to the God who made us and brought us together. My children did not know this song before our friends introduced it to them, and now I hear it being hummed around the house from time to time. It's a catchy tune, and I'm always happy when it gets stuck in my head. The lyrics, and the experience of making music with others, remind me that beauty and friendship are God's gifts.

Non nobis, Domine, non nobis
Sed nomini tuo da gloriam.
(Not to us, Lord, not to us,
But to thy name give the glory.)

Chapter 4 Questions

1. What kinds of music do you enjoy?
2. How often do you sing or play along with music?
3. Can you identify any themes common to the music you love?
4. What were your experiences of music making when you were young?
5. Did any adults or childhood friends discourage your musical contributions?
6. Would you like to feel more confident in your musical abilities?
7. What happens when you ask Jesus to accept your song?
8. Scripture says Jesus sang hymns with his disciples (see Mt 26:30). What do you think his voice sounded like?

9.   What time of day would work well to sing with the children in your life?

CHAPTER 5

Praying with Silence

The LORD will fight for you;
you have only to keep still.
—**Exodus 14:14**

[Jesus] woke up, rebuked the
wind, and said to the sea,
"Quiet! Be still!" The wind
ceased and there was great
calm.
—**Mark 4:39**

A grade school teacher is on recess duty. She hears the chatter of a group of girls nearby, the cheerful shouts of children playing soccer, the squeals of the little ones on the slides. The teacher bends down to attend to a boy with a small scrape on his knee when she suddenly realizes the playground has gone silent. No more noise. Her reaction: dread.

If we're honest, we'll agree that silence tends to have this effect on us. Silence can fill us with panic. We are uncomfortable with silence in conversations; we feel compelled to speak, to *produce* something. Silence can make us feel dumb, literally and figuratively: Don't we have anything to say?

Silence.

Probably this chapter should be comprised only of blank pages. Imagine that! Opening a book to a new chapter and finding empty page after empty page. What would our reaction be to a blank, "silent" book? Our first reaction, most likely, would be to think, *Something is wrong—there's been a mistake.* We presume books will contain words, after all, or at least pictures. People expect words (and pictures and soundtracks) not only in books but everywhere. Very rarely do we escape aural or visual stimuli. Perhaps it is only in sleep that we encounter silence, stillness. A great deal of research suggests that even there, though, in the cozy quiet of our beds, the commotion we absorb all day long disrupts our sleep and prevents us from gaining the full benefits of deep, silent rest.

Silence in Scripture

Scripture, on the other hand, is filled with silence. Paradoxically, the Word of God often calls us to wordlessness. In numerous passages, the gospels describe how Jesus goes off on his own to pray. Several times, after healing someone or revealing a profound mystery, Jesus asks others to remain silent.

Consider this encounter between Jesus and a leper:

> When Jesus came down from the mountain, great
> crowds followed him. And then a leper approached,
> did him homage, and said, "Lord, if you wish, you
> can make me clean." He stretched out his hand,
> touched him, and said, "I will do it. Be made clean."
> His leprosy was cleansed immediately. Then Jesus
> said to him, "See that you tell no one, but go show
> yourself to the priest, and offer the gift that Moses
> prescribed; that will be proof for them." (Mt 8:1–4)

Why would Jesus tell the man—who is probably
bursting with gratitude and joy—to remain silent? Jesus
urges the man to use no words but to show himself to
the priest and to offer the sacrifice outlined in Leviticus.
Astonishingly, the leper's account ends right there in Matthew's gospel. We hear nothing more of this man; we never
watch him approach the priest. Jesus imposes silence on
the leper, and the gospel falls silent as well.

In this silence, I find myself aching to know what
happened next. Did the healed man indeed present himself
according to the Law? Did he tell anyone else? Was he welcomed back into his home? Did he remain free of disease?
How and when did he eventually die?

The parallel account of this healing in Mark's gospel
offers some answers:

> The man went away and began to publicize the
> whole matter. He spread the report abroad so that
> it was impossible for Jesus to enter a town openly.

He remained outside in deserted places, and people kept coming to him from everywhere. (Mk 1:45)

Numerous commentaries on this scripture draw the logical conclusion that Jesus had admonished the man to be silent because he knew what would happen: the crowds would swell and complicate the circumstances of his preaching ministry. It makes sense that Jesus would want to keep a lid on such a dramatic physical cure in order to avoid the hassle of spectacle-seeking crowds. The leper's silence helps Jesus.

I can't help wondering, though, whether Jesus prescribed silence for the man's own sake. Jesus' ministry always put others' needs before his own, after all, so perhaps the leper was the one who needed silence. Jesus himself prayed quietly in many places throughout the gospels. He might have been trying to share the gift of silence with the man he healed. Jesus' final gift to the leper might have been silence itself, which offers peace and perspective.

Silence can be a powerful place to encounter God. Consider Elijah's experience in the first book of Kings. Elijah recognizes God, not in wind, earthquake, or fire, but in a soft, silent breeze:

> [Elijah] came to a cave, where he took shelter. But the word of the LORD came to him: Why are you here, Elijah? He answered: "I have been most zealous for the LORD, the God of hosts, but the Israelites have forsaken your covenant. They have destroyed your altars and murdered your prophets by the sword. I alone remain, and they seek to take my life."

> Then the LORD said: Go out and stand on the mountain before the LORD; the LORD will pass by. There was a strong and violent wind rending the mountains and crushing rocks before the LORD— but the LORD was not in the wind; after the wind, an earthquake—but the LORD was not in the earthquake; after the earthquake, fire—but the LORD was not in the fire; after the fire, a light silent sound. When he heard this, Elijah hid his face in his cloak and went out and stood at the entrance of the cave. (1 Kgs 19:9–13)

As the story continues, the Lord speaks to Elijah again and explains to him how he would save the faithful Israelites from destruction.

This story has fascinated me since the moment I first heard it as a young girl. Brief as it is, it thrills me to hear how the Lord seeks out Elijah, speaks to him, strengthens him. Nothing less than the salvation of the Jewish people was at stake. Prophets of Baal were hunting Elijah. He felt desperate, and terribly alone. I imagine he felt like an utter failure as a prophet of the Lord. The prophet sought the Lord at this chaotic moment and found him—in silence.

In his gorgeous oratorio *Elijah*, Mendelssohn captures Elijah's silent encounter with God in the section "Behold! God the Lord passed by." It might seem contradictory that a huge choral work could provide the listener with an experience of silence, but Mendelssohn does just that. The choir sings energetically about the wind breaking apart the mountains and the earthquake heaving the seas and shaking the earth. The orchestra and choir work up to a frenzy imitating the ensuing fire, the sound swelling and building.

Then they stop.

Just a few instruments carry along in tranquil, sustained notes until the voices reemerge softly: "And after the fire there came a still, small voice / and in that still voice, onward came the Lord." Paul Wagner's website, *Music with Ease*, reflects on this moment in Mendelssohn's music: "And onward sings the chorus in low, sweet, ravishing tones to the end . . . a double chorus of majestic proportions."[1]

The chorus sings repeatedly of the "still, small voice," alternately swelling and falling in volume, and finally closing in gentle softness. Interestingly, it feels as though the song ends not with the last notes from the musicians but with the huge silence we notice as the song fades away. Mendelssohn's music gives us an experience with sound, thrilling us and ultimately leading us to crave the decrescendo and its soulmate: the ensuing silence. Musical works, like life in general, are geared toward sound. *Elijah* shows us how excellent musicians, like peaceful, prayerful souls, are people who make good use of silence.

Practicing Silence

Most parents and teachers don't need to be convinced that silence is therapeutic, that it is a sacred place to encounter God. Modern society is loud and distracting, but our children are louder! I grew up with six brothers in a lively,

Italian-Irish mixed family. When the scrapping and holler-
ing reached a certain level, my mom used to cry out above
the din: "Let us speak of the Christ child!" This exclama-
tion never did, to my recollection, generate a conversation
about the Nativity, but it usually put a lid on the crazy.
People who swore they'd never imitate their parents inev-
itably imitate their parents, right? Thus I now roar above
the noise my own children make, though with a different
tag line. I shout out the Hebrew term for the formless void
described before creation in Genesis: *tohu v'bohu*! I wonder
what my children will one day holler to their own children
to call for quiet.

Childhood is not usually associated with silence, but
even very young children can learn to practice silence and
to crave it. Mother Teresa wrote this about silence: "In the
silence of the heart God speaks. If you face God in prayer
and silence, God will speak to you. . . . Souls of prayer are
souls of great silence."[2] One mom I love keeps close to
her heart the kind of silence Mother Teresa describes. Her
six-year-old son struggles with severe anxiety issues, so she
often asks me to pray that her son will know God's quiet
peace, that silence will enter his body, mind, and heart,
and refresh him.

Silence takes practice. Since children are especially
squirmy, praying with silence has to be a gradual process. It
helps to talk together as a family about the importance of
silence. Reading the passages from the gospels or 1 Kings
that were mentioned above might help contextualize the
long and sacred tradition of encountering God in silence.
After the family (or classroom) agrees to give silence a try,
all it takes is about forty-five seconds of silence—honestly!

1. Plan to be silent with your children for as long as is peaceful—maybe start with thirty seconds, then grow to forty-five seconds, then a minute.
2. Begin the silence by focusing on a single image (Jesus as the Good Shepherd, for example) or a phrase ("I love you, Jesus").
3. Encourage your children to keep that image or phrase in mind while they listen in their silent hearts for God's love.

Our family likes to switch up dinnertime prayer during Advent, a season of stillness. Instead of launching into our traditional Grace before Meals prayer, during those four weeks of Advent we begin the meal in silence. After everyone has situated themselves around the table, we light the Advent candles, turn off the lights, and sit in silence for a few moments. Because we are so accustomed to praying aloud, and because our days surround us with noise, the silent Advent prayer stuns us all. I find myself breathing deeper in those still seconds before the lights go back on. It's no monastery around our place, so even brief encounters with silence affect us powerfully.

When children succeed at praying in silence, even for thirty seconds, they might object that they didn't hear God. An astute second grader once snarled, "My heart doesn't have any ears!" How true! Children can sniff out fraud quickly, so it's important for adults to reassure them that praying in silence is real work and that a real person is listening: God the Father, Son, and Holy Spirit.

Praying in silence, and learning how to listen to God's unique voice, takes time. It might be helpful to remind children how much practice it takes to become potty trained or to learn how to tie shoes or ride a bike. It's always possible that a child will immediately receive a clearly audible and distinct message in prayer. More likely, it will take a while to develop the habit of dialogue with the divine.

Children are concrete thinkers, so "listening with the heart" might not be a helpful model when we first introduce them to praying with silence. Instead, we can encourage these children not necessarily to expect an inner conversation but simply to enjoy the silence itself. Some concrete thinkers might like to experiment with different kinds of listening, of paying attention, outside of the silent prayer time. Children who are looking for God to respond to their silent prayers can seek signs of God's action in various ways:

- through the caring actions of others
- through the kind words of others
- through the words of the Church, especially in the liturgy
- through scripture, the Word of God

Children might also consider that hearing nothing, simply sitting in utter stillness and silence, is a gift. We don't always have to be talking and listening to others talk, even "in our hearts." Sometimes, silence is its own reward. We needn't be distressed or unsatisfied by it. In our over-scheduled, technology-saturated culture, children may grow to love silence, where they can encounter stillness, peace, and God's loving care.

Silence in Conversation

Diana Senechal, PhD, a former New York City public school educator and curriculum advisor, explains: "We must understand the value of both speaking up and refraining from speech. We must, moreover, choose our speech well, so that we are not simply babbling. We must be capable of silence, so that we have a choice."[3] Choosing to be silent requires courage and freedom. Children who cultivate the habit of praying with silence feel more comfortable both in conversation and in silence.

In an interview about her book *Republic of Noise: The Loss of Solitude in Schools and Culture*, Senechal observed that she sees adults "having great difficulty sitting with a book for a long time, or with a pad of paper. They want to have the stimulus right nearby—they want access to their e-mail, they want access to their text messages no matter what they're doing. . . . You see people holding their phones in all situations—at a concert or when having dinner with a friend—so they can check that they don't miss anything."[4] In the classroom, children acquire the same obsession with stimulation:

> Students don't learn how to handle moments of doubt, or moments of silence, or moments where they have to struggle with a problem and they can't produce something right on the spot. So, the students themselves come to expect to be put to work at every moment. If you want to give them something more difficult, you have to expect a little uncertainty. You have to expect a little bit of silence

. . . where students may have a chance to wrestle with something . . . where the answer is not immediately apparent.[5]

Moments of silence, even awkward moments, are opportunities for growth and encounter. We may feel vulnerable in silence because it is so unpredictable. Our good and gracious God, however, does his greatest work in unpredictable ways. He became a human person, suffered, died, and rose from the dead. He meets us where we are, especially when we are vulnerable.

Another practical way to pray with silence is to try to be a listener more than a speaker in conversation from time to time. This goes beyond the negative virtue of silence captured in the adage, "If you don't have anything nice to say, don't say anything at all." Silence is not merely the absence of rudeness; silence is a disposition of peace and generosity.

Families hoping to practice more silence throughout the day might shift their dinnertime discussions from "What did you do today?" to "What did you hear today?" Fascinating! Some children are naturally more introverted and observant, so shifting the conversation in this way can celebrate their strengths.

To be honest, I am perhaps the world's least observant person. One of my closest friends affectionately calls me "oblivious." With no natural inclination to attentiveness, I have to remind myself constantly throughout the day to *pay attention* to people and situations around me. Praying with silence helps. Choosing sometimes to listen rather than speak, to observe rather than act, helps me cultivate silence in my heart and, in the stillness, recognize my Lord. We can encourage our children to practice prayerful silence in this way. Striving for casual goals might be helpful. Set aside time at the end of the class day, at dinner, or at night prayer for each family member to share a certain number of observations, perhaps two or three, from the day. Knowing that I get to report three things I paid attention to in a given day would certainly help me practice more silence than I would without that challenge. Children who practice silence in this way may experience the glory of what St. Paul describes in his letter to the Philippians:

> If there is any encouragement in Christ, any solace in love, any participation in the Spirit, any compassion and mercy, complete my joy by being of the same mind, with the same love, united in heart, thinking one thing. Do nothing out of selfishness or out of vainglory; rather, humbly regard others as more important than yourselves, each looking out not for his own interests, but [also] everyone for those of others. Have among yourselves the same attitude that is also yours in Christ Jesus. (2 Phil 2:1-5)

Children may not often hear that they should "regard others as more important" than themselves. Our self-esteem culture recoils at such a thought, but we are disciples of Christ Jesus. We know the liberating truth of humility. Practicing silence, praying in silence, can lead us closer to

Jesus' Heart, which is meek, humble, observant, patient, glorious, and sacred.

My son Jack learned a lifelong lesson about silence from his third grade teacher. Tammy St. John is a peaceful, beautiful woman who has a talent for helping children experience the good behavior she expects of them. I once happened to be in the classroom at the end of a school day, so I watched the students engage in what St. John called "Compliments." As the students lined up to file out of the classroom, they passed a star-tipped wand among themselves. Any child who had a compliment to pay to another student asked for the wand, thus getting a turn to speak.

What I heard made joyful tears well up in my eyes: these eight- and nine-year-olds took turns identifying silent deeds they had observed in their classmates during the day. Their daily practice of Compliments had attuned their eyes and hearts to look for things that normally escape notice. Here are some examples:

- "I would like to compliment Jacob for working on his math even though the word problems were hard today."
- "I would like to compliment Alexandra for opening the door for a 4–K student who was carrying a lot of books."
- "I would like to compliment Caitlin who didn't get a turn on the tire swing at recess, even though she was waiting in line. When the bell rang, she didn't complain or get angry."

Jack's school has a rich tradition of character formation. The daily morning assemblies often focus on moral behavior, where students pick up practical tips for treating others with kindness and respect. St. John's Compliments activity makes those moral lessons sink deeply into the children's hearts. They experience what it feels like to listen and watch from time to time. They encounter the quiet peace that comes with noticing and encouraging others in small ways. St. John told me that she looks forward to these last five minutes of class each day.

"It is amazing," she says, "how these kids get it that we are complimenting others for who they are and what they do as people—*not* for what they have (clothes, a cool backpack, or even pretty eyes, etc.). I also love to see what the kids remember from the day, and I am always pleasantly surprised when they mention something that happened at a special or a recess when there isn't close adult supervision. Finally, I *love* seeing how students are more eager to give a compliment than receive one."[6]

Compliments helps children practice silence and so does St. John's own example: she never trumpeted the marvelous success of her inspiring activity. She was, in fact, silent about Compliments. I might never have encountered this brilliant exercise had I not happened to be in the classroom that afternoon.

Silence in Deeds

Children love positive reinforcement. As a matter of fact, adults do, too. I certainly haven't outgrown the pleasure of hearing that my work makes a difference. Matthew's gospel gives us Jesus' thoughts about this:

> [But] take care not to perform righteous deeds in order that people may see them; otherwise, you will have no recompense from your heavenly Father. When you give alms, do not blow a trumpet before you, as the hypocrites do in the synagogues and in the streets to win the praise of others. Amen, I say to you, they have received their reward. But when you give alms, do not let your left hand know what your right is doing, so that your almsgiving may be secret. And your Father who sees in secret will repay you. (Mt 6:1–4)

Jesus asks us to do good works in secret, in silence. Parents and teachers know how important positive reinforcement is, but eventually children can learn to love doing good for its own sake.

How can we pray with silence? We can get excited about doing small things for others, such as picking up the playroom or making a sibling's bed without being asked. These deeds are even better when we don't mention them.

Many classrooms and families already encourage silent deeds in the form of "Secret Santa." Secret Santa is an excellent model for children because it accommodates children's attention spans and provides an experience of positive reinforcement in the form of delayed gratification. The obvious start and end dates of Secret Santa season make the period of do-gooding endurable. Anticipation of the final unmasking ceremony keeps the benevolent adrenaline pumping.

We can expand the Secret Santa model and guietly make life better for others. Inspired by Jesus' words in Matthew 6:1–4, we can challenge ourselves and our children. All year long, we can try to "do small things with great love," as Mother Teresa said.

St. Thérèse of Lisieux talked about silent deeds this way in her autobiography: "I prefer the monotony of obscure sacrifice to all ecstasies. To pick up a pin for love can convert a soul." It may seem far-fetched to think picking up a pin can save a soul, but Thérèse trusted Jesus to transform and multiply any tiny offering like he did with a little boy's loaves and fishes in the gospel. Our small, secret deeds are like tools God can use to construct his Kingdom.

In my imagination, dinner conversations in heaven always mention the good others have done for us in imitation of Jesus. The blessed souls around the table speak with joy and gratitude as they proclaim the wonderful deeds of Jesus and his followers. I can imagine this easily because I have tasted it already; God and neighbor have been lavish with me. At one point early on in our marriage, my husband, David, and I were in financial crisis. David had been unemployed for months, and we were expecting our fourth baby in four years. We searched under couch cushions to find change to pay the rent. At the end of one month when we were going to have to short the landlord, an envelope arrived in the mail.

The only writing, inside or out, was our name and address on the front of the envelope. No return address, no note. Contained in the envelope was a twenty-dollar bill, enough to cover the gap. Twenty dollars may not seem like a lot of money, but it meant the world to us that month.

I look forward to the day in heaven when Jesus will introduce me to our silent benefactor and give me the opportunity to proclaim his or her great deed at the heavenly banquet table. And, of course, everyone at the table will discuss how that silent act of charity was just a modest imitation of the great silent deed Jesus performed at Calvary.

We all need to practice silence because we're so unused to the quiet. Let's practice silence with our children so we can learn to listen to Jesus in our hearts, where he comes to us so intimately.

Chapter 5 Questions

1. When and where do you encounter silence?
2. How do you feel when you are surrounded by silence?
3. Some people describe the experience of silence in God's presence as the "Cloud of Unknowing." How does your experience of silence resonate with that description?
4. Why would you like your children to learn how to quiet themselves?

CHAPTER 6

Praying with Reflection

Probe me, God, know my
heart;
try me, know my thoughts.
—**Psalm 139:23**

And Mary kept all these things,
reflecting on them in her heart.
—**Luke 2:19**

Children need to know, really know, that prayer works. Prayer *is* work that has real consequences.

We often feel the instinct to pray at peak moments in life—either ecstatic or agonizing moments—and that's a gift. We also need to remember to return to prayer after those peak moments have passed. That's where reflection comes in. In his recent book *Three Moments of the Day: Praying with the Heart of Jesus*, Fr. Christopher S. Collins, S.J., devotes an entire section to the power of memory, the power of reflecting on the ways we have tried to walk with Christ in any given day. "Simply remembering what has already happened and how God has already been active in one's day makes the soul more attentive to God's presence and care in ordinary, day-to-day living."[1]

We can very easily become fragmented people, people spread thin to accommodate the overwhelming number of activities, duties, car trips, devices, and relationships we manage each day. Even J. R. R. Tolkien's celebrated hobbit Bilbo Baggins admitted to feeling like this in the *Lord of the Rings*: "I feel thin, sort of stretched, like butter scraped over too much bread." Reflection helps us be more attentive in our coming and going. Reflective prayer helps us see that we really are one and the same person at the store, behind the wheel, in the office, at the changing table, and in our bed at the end of each day.

Who Am I?

Reflection helps us recollect ourselves and re-collect what feel like fragmented pieces of ourselves. One of my favorite moments in *Les Misérables* is when dire circumstances force Jean Valjean to reflect on who he is and how his identity must inform his actions. In the Schönberg-Boublil musical version of this exquisite novel, Valjean asks, "Who am I?" over and over again.

At the song's spectacular climax, Valjean practically screams out his prison numbers, coming to terms at last with the truth about himself. All the pieces of his life must be accounted for, must be integrated into one. He has been a convict and fugitive; he is now a wealthy and respected mayor. Nevertheless, he is now and always a sinner loved by God. Nothing about his past or present can escape the loving gaze of God: "My soul belongs to God, I know," he sings. Thus Valjean's process of reflection brings the diverse parts of his life into a coherent whole, and he knows how to respond to the difficult situation currently testing his character.

This poignant scene in *Les Misérables* came to mind when I read the September 30, 2013, interview between Pope Francis and Fr. Antonio Spadaro, S.J., published by the Jesuit magazine *America*. During this interview, Spadaro goes off script and, referring to the pope's given name, asks a disarming question: "Who is Jorge Mario Bergoglio?" Silence. Then Pope Francis's response: "I am a sinner whom the Lord has looked upon."[2] The article, alas, does not say whether the pope stood up to sing these words at the top of his voice à la Jean Valjean. Probably he did not, but the pope's statement is every bit as powerful.

Knowing the truth about ourselves—that we are not perfect, but that our perfect Father loves us with a passion—provides perspective and helps us get on with the work of each day. John 3:16, sports fans' most famous Bible verse, celebrates this truth. God loves each one of us so much that he sent his Son to be one like us in everything but sin. Even though humans sin and die, Jesus Christ offers us eternal life. This is who we are. Reflective prayer helps us ponder this truth in our hearts. Sharing reflective prayer with children gives them the perspective and confidence they need to make good choices more often, and to grow as disciples of the Lord of love.

Praying with reflection enhances the life of individuals as well as of communities. Any corporate executive will affirm the critical importance of crafting a mission statement or reflecting on the vision of the organization. Families and schools have "corporate" identities as well, and reinforcing that identity is part of the reflection process. I've heard many parents discuss strategies to help children cope with disparities they see between friends' families and their own. Children are excellent at spotting differences, and reflection helps them accept their unique identity.

When I was young, I used to run into the pediatrician's waiting room to get to the magazine rack. Desperately, I would search for the new issue of *Highlights* magazine so I could flip to the "Double Check" page to scour the differences between two nearly identical pictures. It was hugely depressing whenever some other kid had already circled all twenty-four differences. In pen. Clearly, my childhood peers enjoyed difference games as much as I did.

Sesame Street, another classic of my youth, capitalizes on children's ability to learn through difference. The song "One of These Things Is Not Like the Other" encourages children to compare and contrast similar objects. Part of how children learn about identity is by recognizing what a thing is not.

Many families make use of this natural skill to reflect on family identity. When toddlers go through a hitting or biting phase, parents reform them by reminding them over and over again, "We don't hit. We use words." This strategy, over time, helps a child differentiate herself from the hitters: *I am peaceful. I use words to solve problems.* Seeing the difference helps children make better choices.

As children grow older, they can feel the sting of being different. Sometimes "the grass is always greener" makes other families' rules seem far more liberal than they really are. "But Rico gets to play Minecraft for three hours!" goes the complaint, when in reality, I know that Rico's mom sets a game timer for thirty minutes.

On the other hand, families really might have drastically different rules and expectations. Praying with reflection can help children accept that. Some of my children's classmates host extravagant birthday parties, with caterers, private laser-tag games, DJs, rented bouncy castles—amazing and magical stuff. After my children got a taste of the bacchanalia, they were hooked. Once in every Urbanski child's life, he or she asked: "Can I please have my party at [insert restaurant name or awesome party place here]?" "Thanks for asking!" began the standard reply, "But Urbanski birthday parties are always at our house. What kind of cake should we make together?"

The Urbanski children did not universally embrace this reply, but the reflective technique helped put the conversation into perspective: *We are the Urbanski family, and these are the options we have.* As my late, great friend Fr. Will Prospero, S.J., was fond of saying, "Compare and despair!" A firm believer in the power of reflective prayer, Fr. Will knew that comparisons bring desolation. Reflective prayer invites us to see ourselves as we truly are: unique, beloved children of God.

Gratitude

Seeing ourselves as unique, beloved children of God changes everything. I realized this dramatically one afternoon on the quiet drive to half-day kindergarten. My four-year-old son Jack broke the silence in the car to ask a question: "Why did God even make us?"

Glancing in the rearview mirror, I saw my son staring out the window at nothing in particular, his little brow furrowed with lines of concentration. "Why did God even make us?" he asked again. After a pause, I responded: "That's a great question, Jack. What made you think about that?" (I learned early on in my parenting career to respond to most children's questions with another question. This technique provides many benefits: it acknowledges a question right away while giving me more time to think; it helps me and the child understand the context of the question; and it counteracts my natural inclination to talk too much, to over-answer what might be a simple question.) "Well," he began, "God is perfect, right? He lives in heaven where everything is perfect all the time. So if God is perfectly happy in heaven, then why bother making us?"

I was so astonished by Jack's thought process that all I wanted to do was pull over and absorb the moment or maybe go to a coffee shop to sit with my little son and his huge question. Because Jack is fond of action stories and has an artistic soul, this was my answer to him that afternoon: "The Bible tells us God is love, right? Love always wants to reach out, to create new things. God's love is so perfect and creative and big, that God just sort of *explodes* people everywhere!"

"Aw, cool!" The answer sufficed, and I heaved a sigh of wonder and relief.

I often think about that conversation with Jack. The entire exchange hangs around in my imagination, even years later, and invites me to reflect. I thought about Jack's question again when I heard Fr. Robert Barron speak at a conference recently. Fr. Barron loves the work of second-century theologian St. Irenaeus. Fr. Barron proposes that "the master idea in Irenaeus's theology is that God has no need of anything outside of himself."[3] In other words, God does not need us.

God does not need us. Instead, God wants us. God thirsts for us. The great adventure of family life is the celebration and exploration of how intensely God wants each of us. St. Augustine says, "God thirsts that we may thirst for him." How breathtaking it is to realize God wants me personally and has a unique plan for me! This passage from Jeremiah puts it another way: "For I know well the plans I have in mind for you . . . plans for your welfare and not for woe, so as to give you a future of hope" (Jer 29:11).

Praying reflectively means sitting with big questions about life, posing those questions *to a person*, to God— the Father, Son, and Holy Spirit.

For a couple thousand years, the Church has set aside entire seasons for reflective prayer: Advent and Lent. These holy times of reflection prepare us for the two major Christian feasts: Christmas and Easter. Both Christmas and Easter show us that God acts not out of duty but out of free love. Just as God did not *have* to create us, he also did not *have* to become one of us nor did he *have* to suffer and die in agony. Creation, the Incarnation, and Christ's death and resurrection are all part of the massively Good News that God loves us for free.

One family I know makes this reflection tangible for their children in Advent by putting up on the wall pictures of each family member as well as an image of Jesus. A sign on the wall proclaims that Jesus himself is "The Best Gift" and encourages the family members to jot down messages under each other's pictures during the four weeks of Advent. The messages relate to the ways Mom, Dad, brothers, and sisters are gifts, simply because God made them. The messages sometimes mention a sister's welcome smile, a brother's kind deed, or Mom's nicely folded piles of clean laundry. This family's cheerful way of praying with reflection is easy to try.

When we think of ourselves and of others as free gifts of God, our natural response is gratitude. Reflective prayer invites and encourages gratitude. We know God has given us everything, even our very selves.

A practical way to respond to the gratitude born of reflection is the good old-fashioned thank-you note. Families looking for ways to keep holy the Sabbath might enjoy a ten- or fifteen-minute thank-you-note session every Sunday. While the littlest children color beautiful pictures, older children, teens, and parents can write one or two thank-you notes. The thank-you note list might be long and very specific after Christmas or a birthday; the other fifty Sundays in the year cry out for creative thinking. Does a teacher need a thank-you note? A cashier at the grocery store? Could the nice man who hands out bulletins at the church doors use a little pick-me-up? How would Dad feel to get a note thanking him for going to work each day?

The people we encounter daily are made in God's image. Reflecting on the gifts they offer inspires creative thankfulness.

The Examen

A kind of reflection St. Ignatius of Loyola insisted on praying each and every day is the examen, also called the evening review. There are lots of ways to pray an evening review, but here are five basic steps common to most versions:

1. I become aware of the presence of our loving God.
2. I say thank you to God for the gifts of this day.
3. I ask the Holy Spirit to guide my prayer and to help me see my day as Jesus sees it.
4. I review the details of my day—emotions I felt, places I went, conversations I had, tasks I accomplished—all of my thoughts, words, and deeds.
5. I resolve to continue along good paths I am following, but to shed negativity and sin as much as possible, asking Jesus for forgiveness and strength.

Reflection helps us pay attention to how God works for us and through us every moment of the day.

Fr. Christopher Collins highlights a way we benefit personally from this kind of reflection. When we review the details of our day, our "remembering takes place in relationship to God who has entered into history and become a person. . . . My life is now within God's life, my story within God's story."[4] The examen leads us to reflect on ourselves every day, reminding us that God is personally interested in every little thing we do, think, or say.

Imagine the examen in terms of social media. I am amazed that more than fifty million people follow the Twitter feeds of celebrities such as Katy Perry and Justin Bieber. Their tweets often relate to their music careers, but frequently followers hear about mundane life details: what shoes they're wearing, how a tennis lesson or a bike ride went, what a friend just said in conversation. More than *fifty million* people make sure to check in on their beloved celebrities every day to delight in the minutiae of their lives. God feels this way about us, and our examen is a little like our Twitter or Instagram accounts. While the whole point of launching an identity into the social media sphere is to attract a ridiculous number of followers, the examen is a more intimate affair: just one human person in contact with God. The level of excitement Twitter generates about the tiny details of a celebrity's life offers a strange glimpse into the intensity of God's interest in each of our lives.

Knowing about God's interest in and love for us changes things. I recently had a conversation with an older gentleman, Hank, who told me about his first grade teacher, a religious sister. This sister must have known the desperate difficulties Hank faced in his broken home.

One day she looked him right in the eyes and said with authority and compassion, "God is *always* with you."

Hank never forgot those words. He often thought of them, especially in his adolescent years when he had plenty of opportunity to choose a destructive path. The words he heard in first grade saved him at those critical moments in his life, because they reminded him of his indestructible connection with his loving God. "God is *always* with you" defined him as a treasured child of God and gave him the courage to choose good.

Children can learn to pray the examen, and they will benefit richly from reflecting on the intimate attentiveness God showers on each of us. God never takes his gaze from us. We remain in existence only because God wills it, because he continues to think of us with love every second of the day. God is interested in everything we do. In God, there are no fragments, no compartments, only wholeness. The examen helps children learn to see their lives in that integrated way.

The Apostleship of Prayer presents the examen in a way children can understand, asking children to imagineth that the review of their day is like watching a movie but not alone. As Fr. Collins reminds us, the examen is always about relationship: our relationships with others and ultimately our relationship with God.[4] That's why we call our review for children "Going to the Movies with God."

Nightly Examen with Children

1. **Hanging Out:** Meet up with God at the movie theater.

   Know that God is with you now. Silently, in your heart, say hello to God: the Father, the Son, and Holy Spirit.

2. **Thanking God for His Gifts:** Grab some popcorn with Abba (Daddy)!

   Let some happy moments from this day pop into your head like popcorn. In your heart, say thank you to your Father for these gifts.

3. **Paying Attention:** Get cozy and ask the Holy Spirit to prepare the movie.

   Get ready to see your thoughts, your words, and your deeds. In your heart, ask the Holy Spirit to show you your day the way God sees it.

4. **Watching Today's Movie:** Relax next to Jesus and watch your day together.

   Let your imagination replay your day. Let your heart react to what you see.

   Helpful hint: Imagine different soundtracks playing along with the movie of your day: cheerful, upbeat music when you see things that are loving, kind, and thankful, and more serious music when you see things that are selfish, mean, or greedy.

   Rember: Jesus was with you all day. What does he think about what you see together?

- How did I get to school this morning? What was the trip like?
- What did I say to people as I arrived at school?
- Which classes or activities did I attend today? How did I participate?
- What were my meals like: the food I ate, the time I spent eating, the people around me?
- Which people did I see and talk to? What did I think about them in my heart?

5. **Making New Plans:** Decide how to act tomorrow.

Ask God to be a part of everything that happens tomorrow. Choose one thing to work on together. Remember, there's always a new movie to make starring you and God. Choose one thing to work on together. Remember, Thank you, God!

Helpful hint: A resolution is a decision about how to behave tomorrow.

- Did you make some bad choices today? Tell God you're sorry.
- Did you make some good choices today? Say, "Thank you, God, for all your goodness to me!"

The movie analogy sticks with children. A child named Peter confirmed this for me this summer, a couple of months after our Apostleship of Prayer Family Retreat. Both my own family and Peter's family had attended this annual retreat on a lake in central Wisconsin. Each night before bedtime, I gathered all the children aged three to eleven to lead them through "Going to the Movies with God." Though the children achieved a remarkable level of quiet, a predictable amount of giggling and squirming is always part of an examen reflection with a large batch of vivacious children. The children on this retreat responded enthusiastically to our nightly "trip to the movies." Even so, I always wonder just how deeply the examen seeds have been planted after only a couple of evenings together.

I saw Peter and his family again a few months later at our diocesan seminary. Bishop Donald Hying celebrated the Mass that day at the seminary, and he preached about the benefits of reflective prayer, specifically, an evening review at the end of each day. After Mass, six-year-old Peter ran up to me and exclaimed, "Did you hear the bishop? He was talking about the Movie!" Bishop Hying had not mentioned "Going to the Movies with God," of course, but Peter connected his nightly habit of reflection, his "Movie," with the words he heard at church. Children like Peter who build a habit of reflective prayer learn to cultivate heartfelt gratitude for the gifts of each day and a stable, personal relationship with the Lord.

Reflecting on the Mystery of God

Some families keep a prayer journal or a prayer jar in their home where family members can draw or write down special prayer intentions. Once a month or so, the family gathers to read through the prayers and consider how

God has responded. This peaceful family time together can help us remember that God does not always answer our requests in the way we imagine, but that he always listens to us and draws close to us in prayer. And as we pray, we grow as disciples of the Lord.

Chapter 6 Questions

1. How often do I step back from my activities and reflect on who I am and why I do what I do?

2. How many minutes could I realistically dedicate to an examen each day, either at lunchtime or in the evening?

3. How would the children in my life benefit from a few minutes of reflective prayer each day?

CHAPTER 7

Praying with the Apostleship of Prayer

But I will call upon God, and
the LORD will save me.
At dusk, dawn, and noon I will
grieve and complain,
and my prayer will be heard.
—**Psalm 55:17–18**

Persevere in prayer,
being watchful in it with
thanksgiving.
—**Colossians 4:2**

Once a month, the Apostleship of Prayer hosts young adults for morning Mass and volunteering at our national offices. All their young children are welcome to spend the morning with my helpers (often my lovely nieces and nephews) and me in the playroom attached to my office. One morning, as I distributed the celebrated Apostleship

of Prayer snack of fruit chews and juice boxes, one preco-
cious three-year-old girl, Sophia, walked right up to me.
She shot her hand up into the air and practically shouted,
"I am sacrificing juice today!"

"Oh, you're making a sacrifice of prayer for someone?" I asked. "Who?"

"My opa [grandpa]! He already had surgery, and my
oma [grandma] is taking care of him. I'm sacrificing my
juice for him."

Ordinarily, little Sophia finds charming ways to
ask for seconds or thirds of the day's snack. Her prayerful sacrifice that day, however, carried her through the
entire morning without complaint. Sophia is an Apostle
of Prayer. At three years of age, she demonstrates that her
small sacrifice on behalf of another has real consequences
in this world.

Apostles of Prayer are believers, of any age, who trust
that God accepts our offerings and transforms them into
grace for others. What a brilliantly practical approach
to living! We can offer as a sacrifice absolutely anything:
abstaining from juice boxes, washing dishes, changing a
diaper, driving to sports practice, smiling sincerely at an
aggravating person, or caring for a chronically ill child or
parent. All of these offerings please God.

God is deeply in love with us and pays attention to
every detail of our days. It makes a lot of sense to make
a point of returning his gaze, of acknowledging how he
creates and sustains us. Even when we feel overwhelmed
and fragmented, offering our daily activities to God helps
us start putting things in order.

The Apostleship of Prayer sprang up in France in 1844. It began when spiritual director and Jesuit father Francis-Xavier Gautrelet wrote a morning offering prayer for the novice Jesuits in his care. These young Jesuits were eager to travel to distant countries to proclaim the Good News of Jesus Christ. The Society of Jesus, of course, has one of the longest formation processes of any religious order; these enthusiastic young men were going nowhere soon, except maybe the library. As his spiritual directees grumbled about philosophy homework, Fr. Gautrelet must have decided prayer was the answer. So he wrote one: the morning offering.

As he presented his offering prayer to the men, Fr. Gautrelet encouraged them: "Be apostles now, apostles of prayer! Offer everything you are doing each day in union with the Heart of our Lord for what He wishes, the spread of the kingdom for the salvation of souls."[1] There is no need to travel to exotic lands to perform heroic deeds for God. Simply *choosing intentionally* to do the work right in front of us (such as philosophy homework) is difficult enough, isn't it? And when we consciously choose to offer our work for the good of others, we imitate Jesus. We join our own humble offerings to his eternal offering, adding our own sacrifices to "what is lacking in the afflictions of Christ" (Col 1:24).

Within forty years of Fr. Gautrelet's morning offering pep talk, more than thirty-five thousand Apostleship of Prayer offices were active around the world, uniting its thirteen million members in daily prayer. (How does something go viral like that, before the digital age?) Pope Leo XIII was impressed with this trending grassroots prayer movement and asked the Apostleship to publicize his own personal prayer intention each month to all its members. A few decades later, another pope, Pius XI, approached the organization to entrust a second prayer intention for the work of the Church around the world, especially in mission territories.

Growing up, I often heard people say they were praying "for the intentions of the Holy Father," but I assumed those prayer intentions were some sort of Vatican secret. Astonishingly, I was well into my twenties before I met the Apostleship of Prayer and learned how they care for and spread the pope's prayer requests.

The minute I heard about the Apostleship's worldwide prayer network, I knew I wanted to be a part of it. I wanted to join my prayers and (sometimes pathetic and little) sacrifices to those of my brothers and sisters around the world. We strugglers, sinners, sojourners—and maybe even saints—unite in prayer each morning. Honestly, sometimes the thing that gets me out of bed in the morning is the knowledge that millions of people are praying for me and that they need my prayers, too.

The Apostleship of Prayer promotes all kinds of prayer but most especially the morning offering and evening review. The morning offering directs all our daily activities to God. As we read in the previous chapter, the evening review looks back at the day, serving as a perfect bookend. Each evening, we consider the ways we lived in the love of the Lord that day, the ways we offered ourselves for others in our thoughts, words, and deeds. While the morning offering prayer anticipates potential encounters of the day ahead, the evening review (or examen, as

St. Ignatius of Loyola called it) reflects on actual interactions. We recall real, concrete people and places, rather like watching a movie of our day, side by side with the friend who loves us most in the world.

The Apostleship of Prayer helps me think of my day as a kind of sandwich: the morning offering and evening review are the bread—thick, hearty, healthy, multigrain slices capable of holding together the messy details of my day. To extend the sandwich metaphor, I often discover that the stuff in between the bread is an astonishing collection of unhealthy fare: junk food (dumb videos), expired cold cuts (rotten things I said to others), candy (Candy Crush binges), and even nonfood items (anxieties or gossiping). Putting a nonfood item—for example, a shoe—into a sandwich makes as much sense as worrying about the future or tearing down a person's character. Sadly, those shoes keep appearing in my sandwiches. Well, healthy or not, all the stuff in my daily sandwich is an opportunity to grow closer to Jesus. Keeping in mind the morning offering, I can entrust my day's events to the Heart of Jesus, who offered himself for the salvation of the world. The bits and pieces of my daily existence can help me enter into spiritual communion with the Lord.

I love these three "moments" of each day: the morning offering, the evening review, and spiritual communion with Jesus in between. Along with its duty to spread worldwide the prayer intentions of the pope, inviting folks into these three moments of the day is the work of the Apostleship of Prayer. Children and adults who live these three moments and pray with the pope build life-giving daily habits of prayer.

Morning Offering

Each morning I ask God to accept the prayers, thoughts, words, actions, joys, and sufferings my day will include. As St. Ignatius of Loyola's Suscipe prayer reminds us, God has given all to me; now I return it. My morning offering helps me be vigilant, attentive to God's action in my daily life. Mindful of my morning offering, I am more likely to seek God in the people and events I encounter. Many evenings I return to my bed, wearied from the day's labor, and realize what I actually offered to God that day was pathetic—sometimes downright mortifying. Providentially, we have a God who demonstrates regularly the power to take disaster, abuse, sin, and shoddy attempts and to transform them, redeem them. That is, of course, the story of our faith; we are disciples of the resurrected Jesus.

The Apostleship of Prayer knows millions of people around the world make a morning offering in some way. Starting my day with this simple prayer gives me confidence that I am part of a global community of individuals connected by the desire to trust in God's providence for everyone. I guess it "takes a village" to get me out of bed. I'm okay with that. I know God loves me as if I am the only person on earth, but I'm awfully glad millions of other people can say that as well.

Children can learn the habit of the morning offering, too. Natural learners, children quickly learn to seek God in their thoughts, words, and deeds. Almost every day I talk to parents looking for ways to make mornings less hysterical, more peaceful. We're searching for practical ways to be more intentional in family prayer life. My proposal: try the morning offering! Try it. Just give it a shot for three days, then five days, then a week. See what happens when the whole family stops. Stops. Stops completely and offers that dawning day back to the one who gave it to us.

This Morning Offering for Children written by the Apostleship of Prayer goes perfectly to the tune of "Amazing Grace." Try singing the prayer—really! Cultivating the habit of the morning offering prayer can inspire us and infuse meaning into our daily activities.

Morning Offering for Children
For love of me you came to earth:
You gave your life for me.
So every day you give me now
I give back happily.

Take all my laughter, all my tears,
Each thought, each word, each deed,
And let them be my all-day prayer
To help all those in need. Amen. [2]

St. Thérèse of Lisieux, one of the most famous members of the Apostleship of Prayer, loved the morning offering. Even at the young age of twelve, Thérèse knew that offering her thoughts, words, and deeds for the good of others really could change the world. Not long after joining the Apostleship of Prayer, Thérèse chose to adopt her "first child," as she called him, a convicted murderer named Henri Pranzini.

Learning from the newspapers about his crimes and unrepentant attitude, Thérèse began sacrificing little things each day for his conversion. After Pranzini met his death at the guillotine, Thérèse learned that God's grace touched Pranzini at the extreme last minute. Just before the blade came down on Pranzini, a priest held out a crucifix to him, which Pranzini kissed three times. Confident that God had used her offerings to touch the heart of a murderer, Thérèse continued to adopt spiritual children for the rest of her short life, thinking of them in her morning offering and remembering them in her sacrifices throughout each day.

When I speak to middle school students about the morning offering, the story of Thérèse and her "first child" makes a dramatic impression on them. They respond in generous and specific ways when I turn the story over to them. They easily recall persons who could benefit by the strength of their prayers.

Middle school students know about suffering. They have suffered themselves, they love people who are in pain and crisis, and they follow devastating news stories. The temptation to despair looms, and its menace can grip our hearts.

I remember one young man, an eighth grader, who had been somewhat disruptive and impolite during my visit to his class. Although he attended a faith-based school, he seemed unenthusiastic about religion, at least on the day of my visit. Clearly the class clown, he found any way possible to draw attention to his shenanigans throughout our prayer time together. Yet, when I asked the class to think of just one person who could benefit from their prayers, he became deadly serious. He looked up at me. With tears in his eyes, he asked if he could offer up his day not for one person but for two. Whatever pain his comedy masked found an antidote in prayer.

What does God have in store for this young man, I wonder? He is clever, well liked, and confident. He had an intimate encounter with God in prayer the day I met him. If he continues to draw strength from the power of personal sacrifice, God could do great things through him. Clearly, this young man already knows suffering. The morning offering and evening review may help him take to heart the words of the prophet Jeremiah: "For I know well the plans I have in mind for you . . . plans for your welfare and not for woe, so as to give you a future of hope" (Jer 29:11). Daily prayer reminds us of God's very good plans for us, even when we feel lost or overwhelmed. The morning offering refreshes our perspective and brings us into personal contact with God, who cares for us perfectly and eternally.

Children tend to love the idea of the morning offering. One reason for this is their desire for independence, their rush to grow up. After all, parents and teachers dictate most of the daily activities for children, which is appropriate, really. The morning offering, however, is a gift only the child can give. No one else can live your day for you. No one else would respond just exactly like you to the things you encounter each day. Children like the idea of offering something absolutely unique.

Interestingly, while most children I encounter feel empowered by the idea that they alone can offer their day in behalf of others, many adults have a negative response.

Specifically, they worry that they have nothing worth offering. A lifetime of suffering, perhaps, has tempted them to believe the whispers of an enemy, the enemy of our human nature whose business is to draw us further away from God. *What do* you *have to offer? You're not good enough. What if you fail? You hypocrite. Why start now? You're pathetic.* The enemy loves to whisper things like this to people who consider growing their prayer lives.

The morning offering encourages us to draw close to the Lord, to offer ourselves like Jesus, to be his hands and feet on earth. *That's* how important we are. We are the Body of Christ in this world. Let's offer everything we have and do, no matter what, to our loving Father.

Many adults I encounter admit they wish they prayed more, but they're too overwhelmed by each day's demands even to *think* about adding prayer to the to-do lists. The morning offering acknowledges this busyness. In fact, the morning offering embraces the to-do lists. The prayer lasts only thirty seconds or so. Once we have offered it, we are free to welcome the rest of our daily tasks and interactions in a spirit of prayer and self-giving. Sure, we'll forget our offering at times—it's not magic. Even so, the morning offering can be exciting and transformative. Each morning, declaring our openness to encountering God in every thought, word, and deed reminds us how vitally important we are to God's loving plan of salvation for the world. Being busy with our daily work means we have more, not less, opportunity to pray effectively, to draw close to our Lord.

Spiritual Communion

Sophia, the little girl mentioned at the beginning of this chapter, already knows her prayer offerings make a difference in the world. In a few years, when she prepares to make her First Communion, she will have the opportunity to see that her offerings imitate the offering of Jesus in his Passion.

St. Paul writes, "Now I rejoice in my sufferings for your sake, and in my flesh I am filling up what is lacking in the afflictions of Christ on behalf of his body, which is the church" (Col 1:24). This verse often shocks scripture readers because we know Jesus is God; his sacrificial offering was perfect. What could be lacking in his afflictions? The answer: *our* free participation in the Cross. In the Eucharist, we remember the perfect sacrifice of Jesus Christ. In our daily lives, we bear witness to Christ in and through our own bodies. Neither Sophia nor I was present at Jesus' crucifixion, but her sacrifice of juice for her grandpa pulls us back in time. No matter how microscopic the scale might be, when I watch Sophia walk away from the juice box queue, I see Jesus offering his life for me.

In *Three Moments of the Day*, Fr. Christopher Collins spends time reflecting on the Catholic liturgy, tying the actions of that universal prayer to the movements in our hearts. Fr. Collins, a dear friend of mine, invites us to see how offering ourselves like Jesus in the three moments of each day parallels the ultimate sacrifice of Jesus commemorated in the liturgy. I read the majority of that book on a plane trip, much to the chagrin of the woman sitting next to me. Try as I might to contain myself, the tears kept flowing.

Fr. Collins's words highlight the connection between our daily offerings and the sacrifice of Jesus on the Cross:

> [At Mass we pray] not only for ourselves gathered at that Mass but also for "the peace and salvation of all the world." That's what is at stake here—the salvation of all the world. And it is accomplished by the sacrifice of Christ on the Cross, re-presented on the altar at every Mass, and the sacrifices of our daily, apparently insignificant lives.
>
> That is the one story, and each one of us is an essential character in that story, all of us gathered around the person of Christ who is at the center. He is the one sent to bring all humanity back to the Father, and we are necessary participants in his mission. The mission plays out every day in each corner of the world that you and I occupy.[4]

As we recall our morning offering at various moments throughout the day, God reminds us that we are an indispensable part of his plan to save the world. Remembering that I am loved, cherished, and irreplaceable unleashed all those tears on the plane (sorry, lady in seat 3B!). Those tears were a gift, an invitation to draw intimately near to the Heart of Jesus and to be in communion with him. Even if I cannot get to Mass every day to commemorate the story of our faith, I can pray for spiritual communion with Jesus. I can commemorate the sacrifice of Jesus by uniting my own big and small sacrifices to his.

In various places throughout his book, Fr. Collins directs the reader in meditative prayer. In his meditation on spiritual communion, Fr. Collins invites readers to imagine the moment in the liturgy when the gifts are presented to the priest and then placed on the altar. Imagine, he says, that our very own hearts are there on the altar with the gifts of bread and wine.

I like to go one step further when imagining spiritual communion on the altar of sacrifice. My heart alone isn't there on the altar as an offering; my body is there, too.

Truly, "the heart" is a satisfying metaphor for the whole person. After all, "wearing your heart on your sleeve" means you hide nothing from the world. Even so, imagining my heart on the altar feels a lot safer than putting my whole body up there. After five children, this bag of bones ain't what it used to be. It's possible that a woman might have a difficult time allowing her body to be placed on the altar, even just in her imagination. There's that whisper again: *You're not good enough.*

Try imagining your own journey to the altar. First of all, where are you in the church? Which seat did you choose? Is it in the front, the middle, or so far in the back that you're practically out the door? As the time to offer the gifts approaches, how do you feel about offering yourself? Are you confident, like Sophia giving up her juice? Are you ashamed? Is there someplace else you'd rather be?

Is there music playing in the church of your imagination? Does the music reflect your own feelings right now?

How do you approach the altar? Are you walking? Striding? Crawling on hands and knees? Are you being carried on a cot by friends?

Once you, your whole body and soul, are on the altar, take a look around. This is a strange vantage point, isn't it? Soak in everything you see. As you hear the priest begin to pray, look at him. He returns your gaze, and you see that it is Jesus. Jesus is the priest, but he is also the offering. He knows what it's like to be where you are now. He looks at you with profound understanding and love. He longs for communion with you. What do you say to Jesus?

Eventually, tell Jesus what you have to offer. Not much, you think? Tell him that. He knows, but he loves to hear it from you. Tell Jesus about all the prayers, thoughts, words, actions, joys, and sufferings you will make available for him to transform just as he transforms bread and wine into his very Body and Blood. Tell Jesus that you want to offer yourself for the salvation of the world just as he did. This is spiritual communion.

Asking to be in spiritual communion with Jesus, all day long, is powerful stuff. Imaginative prayer can help us cherish the intimacy communion offers and help us be more intentional throughout the day. Children learn how to make offerings by watching the generous adults in their lives. Children who know Jesus make the connection between our own sacrifices and his. It can start with something as small as a four-ounce juice box.

Evening Review

The morning offering invites us to offer our days for the good of others. As this habit of offering draws us more and more into spiritual communion with Jesus, we see our own hearts grow. Like all "best practices," the practices of the morning offering and spiritual communion become increasingly effective when we take the time to reflect on how things are going. This is where the evening review comes in handy.

On December 3, 2014, the Apostleship of Prayer celebrated its 170th anniversary. To commemorate the event, the international office, headquartered in Rome, released their "Recreation Documents." Pope Francis himself contributed to the documents. The primary document highlights the importance of the evening review: "At the end of the day, in a moment of silence, I ask the Holy Spirit to show me in which ways Jesus has been with me during this day, and I thank him. I ask myself in which ways I have been available to his mission, and I also thank him. I look at how I have been an obstacle to his work in me, and I ask that in his mercy he may come and transform my heart."[5]

One night not too long ago, when I was deep in the potty-training years, I was trying to pray my evening review. The day had been miserable. Circumstances, and my own reactions to those circumstances, stank. We've probably all had days like this. I had hollered at children who honestly deserved milder reprimands; I had avoided important work; and I had welcomed my husband home with neither a smile nor an expression of interest in his day but with an icy declaration that it was his turn to be the parent.

Not so pretty.

My evening review reminded me that I had offered that day's loathsome thoughts, words, and deeds to God. Eek. Feeling ashamed, I began to look back at the events of the day. I recalled the grossest crisis of the day, when my potty-training daughter sloshed the contents of her potty all over the walls and floor of the hallway. I had been changing the baby's diaper when she had (finally!) had a potty success on her own. In rhapsodic jubilation, she called to me: "Mom! Come and see! Mom! Look what I did! Oh my gosh, Mom!"

"The baby's on the changing table, honey! I'll come in a minute! I can't leave him now or he'll fall off. *Please* stay there! I'll be there just as soon as I can!"

Her triumph, however, could not be compromised by delay. She picked up the potty and ran as fast as she possibly could, waving it recklessly above her head.

What could I do? She had done something truly remarkable for a toddler. She had done her best! Here she was, presenting (sloppily) the fruits of her labor to me. I thanked her for her "offering" and set about cleaning it up.

As I recalled that episode in my evening review, I realized that my own offering that day smelled a lot like my daughter's. I probably hadn't done my best, but I often did everything I possibly could. In that quiet moment of prayer at the end of the day, I smiled as I imagined what my heavenly Father has to do to clean up after my offerings some days. If even *I* can smile and accept the dubious offering of my toddler, focusing on what she did well, then how much more lovingly does our merciful God look on our imperfect offerings? As we saw in the chapter on praying with reflection, one of the steps of the evening review involves asking for forgiveness. God helped me to ask for forgiveness that evening. You can bet I also asked for the strength to make a better offering the next day.

Children amaze me with their ability to pray the evening review. As we saw in the previous chapter, the Apostleship of Prayer teaches children the five-step evening review, calling it "Going to the Movies with God," and the analogy works.

One of my favorite Apostleship of Prayer stories was relayed to me a few days after I visited a parish to teach the children how to pray the evening review. I explained the idea, and the children discussed why reflecting back on the day is a helpful skill to learn. Then we went through the steps of "Going to the Movies with God" and actually practiced praying the examen. A week or so later, one of the moms of those children contacted me to share what happened the evening after my visit. She tucked her son in to bed and kissed him goodnight, then headed toward the bedroom door. Her son called out to stop her: "Mom! Wait! Don't you want to watch my movie with me?"

Jesus said we each must come into the kingdom of God as a little child (Mk 10:15). Children themselves, then, surely have something to teach us adults about how to prepare for the kingdom of God. A child nursing in her mother's arms is the very picture of dependence and trust. Maybe that natural inclination of children to depend on and trust the adults who care for them is what adults must rediscover to find the way to the kingdom of God. The practice of the evening review reveals, day after day, how God provides for us. It's not always easy to recognize God's plan, much less to accept it.

However, the evening review encourages us to marvel at how God always, always cares for us. No one has ever cared for us the way God does. Children who love the adults in their lives the way we ought to love God help us see why Jesus told us to become like little children.

With natural trust still intact, children offer powerful prayers. A child who knows that God will always take care of her has the power to love others with the Heart of Jesus. A child who knows that God is always with him can live a joyful life. The Apostleship of Prayer "sandwich—" the morning offering, spiritual communion, and evening review—can be a mighty tool in a child's interior life. What a gift it is to help a child unlock the power of the heart, where God dwells in each of us!

Praying with the Pope!

A Jesuit, a son of St. Ignatius, Pope Francis knows the habit of the evening review. He builds time in his day to feed his habit of prayer. I will never forget the prayer-filled, electrifying silence in St. Peter's Square on the night of his election, when he bowed his head and asked us all to pray for him. On his one-year anniversary in March

2014, he echoed that moment, saying simply: "Pray for me."

Each month, Pope Francis entrusts to the Apostleship of Prayer two prayer intentions close to his heart. Since the 1800s, this is what popes do. Every pope since the eighteenth century's Pope Leo XIII has asked to be a part of the prayer movement by submitting prayer requests to us. We are the "pope's prayer group."

Long before 2015 rolled in, Pope Francis submitted his prayer intentions for 2015 to the international Apostleship of Prayer office in Rome, who sent them along to my office in the original Italian. I was thrilled to be a part of the team in our US office who translated them into English. We checked in frequently with other national offices to compare translations and then submitted them to Rome for approval. Once they are approved each year, Rome distributes our translation to Apostleship of Prayer offices in every English-speaking country in the world.

I get to adapt the pope's prayers into simple language children will absorb. I also write reflections and design related activities for children to share with their families. Children understand that the pope knows a lot of people around the world; he sees areas of particular need. The pope gives the Apostleship of Prayer his two intentions each month, and children who learn the art of the morning offering are happy to join him in prayer.

I love that the Apostleship of Prayer's monthly reflections and activities for children follow the pope's prayer life. Praying with Pope Francis means praying with an informed and insightful leader. In any given day, the Holy Father could meet with international journalists, leaders from other faith traditions, janitorial workers, and a prime minister or two.

Faithfully remembering the pope's prayer intentions each month expands a child's worldview. By the end of a calendar year, children have considered twenty-four diverse groups of people and global issues. Creating twenty-four reflections and activities for children is possibly my favorite part of serving with the Apostleship of Prayer, largely because I love picturing the children who will encounter the reflections with the adults who care for them.

In the context of prayer, these children will consider people such as scientists and prisoners, realities such as unemployment and human trafficking, and places such as Latin America and Asia. Children who learn to pray for the needs of others, needs the pope feels deeply in his own heart, grow in confidence that God listens to our prayers. These children also grow in openness to new people, realities, and places—and to the idea that God might be calling them to serve in one of these areas of need. I am convinced that praying with the pope can help children discover their vocations and respond generously to God's call. In the meantime, the habit of daily prayer encourages children to be sensitive to the needs of those around them0 and to be patient with themselves. Encountering God every day in a personal way expands our minds and hearts.

In 1994, the 150th anniversary of the Apostleship of Prayer, Pope John Paul II (who was himself a member) praised the work of the association:

As the dawn of the third millennium approaches a world in which many sectors have become quite pagan, it is obvious how urgent it is for members of the Apostleship of Prayer to be involved in the service of the new evangelization. For Christ has come to preach the Good News to the poor, and the Apostleship of Prayer has always considered itself a form of popular piety for the masses. As such it has performed an important service during the past hundred and fifty years by giving new life to people's awareness of how valuable their lives are to God for the building up of His Kingdom.[6]

Amen. God values our lives. He calls us to build up his kingdom. He calls us to prayer. And Pope Francis is calling us, too. Let's pray with the pope! He's praying with us.

"A Pathway with Jesus in Apostolic Readiness," one of the international Apostleship of Prayer's recreation documents, reminds me of the mission of the association: "The Apostleship of Prayer is above all a way to cultivate an interior readiness to participate in Christ's mission. The source and the model for this readiness is Jesus who gives out his life for us and to us, continuously made present in the Eucharist. Receiving his life leads us, in grateful response, to offer our lives every day to the Father."[7] Our mission empowers and enlightens children and the adults who care for them.

Chapter 7 Questions

1. Do you ever feel overwhelmed and exhausted by all the things you do each day?

2. Do you ever wish you prayed more?

3. Does praying more seem impossible simply because you're so busy?

4. Does the Apostleship of Prayer "sandwich" (morning offering, spiritual communion, and evening review) sound like a realistic way to pray more?

5. What appeals to you about remembering the prayer intentions of the pope?

6. How would the children in your life respond to uniting in prayer with the Apostleship of Prayer: praying the "sandwich" and praying with the pope?

Afterword

Whoever loves me will keep my
word, and my Father will love
him, and we will come to him
and make our home with him.
—John 14:23

My younger brother John used to make homes for his stuffed animals. One of his favorite dolls was Bucky the Beaver from *The Get-Along Gang*. John used empty tissue boxes, paper towel rolls, cardboard, and a whole lot of markers to create a cozy home for Bucky. Lots of children enjoy creating homes like my brother did. Some use Legos or blocks, some use tree branches or elaborate store-bought sets, and others simply use their imaginations. We have a human instinct to build, to nest, to draw the pieces and people of our lives together in one place. We love *home*.

We parents get to make homes for our children. Many generous parents I know make homes also for foster children, stepchildren, and adopted children. Teachers and other adults often provide a loving home away from home, which is especially critical for children who know the pain of homelessness, broken homes, unstable or harmful parent relationships. Our desire to make a home, and protect it, comes from God. God is a home builder.

Prayer can make a lasting home. This is not just a figure of speech; God actually dwells in us. As the verse above from the Gospel of John says, "Whoever loves me will keep my word, and my Father will love him, and we will come to him and make our home with him" (Jn 14:23). God, Creator of everything, wants to become tiny, to dwell within each of us. *How* this is possible I do not fully understand. That it *is* possible I know from personal experience. Prayer helps me know. Prayer helps us touch God and stay in touch. Prayer is a conversation, a relationship, a way of life. We can find all sorts of ways to pray in daily life—this book explored seven interesting ways. The desire to pursue any or all of them is itself a gift from God. The instant we begin communicating with God, or wondering if we should, we are already in prayer.

Meeting children for the first time is always interesting. Imagine meeting a child people describe as "athletic." How about "popular"? How would you feel knowing you were about to meet an "intelligent" child? A "prayerful" child? The idea of prayerful children intrigues me, helping me picture young people who know they are created by God. A loving God. A personal God who is interested in every detail of their lives. A God who has beautiful plans of hope for them. Children who know that God will always take care of them have the power to love others with the Heart of Jesus. Children who know, deep in their hearts, that God is always with them can live lives of gratitude and joy. Yes, these are the same children who will sometimes make bad choices, break our hearts, and bewilder us, but their personal habit of prayer will keep them connected to heaven, even in the tough times.

Let's pray for our children. Let's pray with our children, encouraging them to have confidence in God's love for them, to return God's love in prayer and service, to give thanks, to cultivate a habit of daily prayer, and to offer each day to God for the good of others.

Eventually, we will no longer remain with our children. Any number of circumstances may begin the separation. Death will complete it, at least on earth. Even then, our perfect gentle Lord will watch over our children for us: "I will not leave you orphans; I will come to you," he says (Jn 14:18). And when Jesus comes to our children, there will be no tears. No, when Jesus comes, our children will know precisely who approaches; they will recognize him from their prayers.

Acknowledgments

Movie credits seem to roll on endlessly these days; I used to marvel at how many people it takes to make a film. After writing this book, I am no longer surprised. What a team we are to produce *Pray with Me*!

Ave Maria Press, thank you for the warm welcome into your family. Bob Hamma, Heidi Hess Saxton, and Stephanie Sibal, thank you. As for you, Jonathan Ryan Weyer, to you I offer my thanks, gratitude, indebtedness, and appreciation.

Educators of the world, unite! You brilliant professionals keep me on my toes: Gini Boyer; Dr. Kathleen Cepelka; Erin Dolan; Stephen Dowling; Martha Ebent; Nancy Gordon; Colleen Hutt; Dr. Maria Keaton; Sr. Christine Kiley, A.S.C.J; Bethany Leonard; Susan McNeil; Gary Pokorney; Linda Pryor; Fr. Erik Ross, O.P.; Nan Ross; Wes Schultz; Sr. Bridget Smith, A.S.C.J.; Tammy St. John; Mary Tretow; Julie Valencia; and David Wacholz.

To my fellow moms who contributed to this project, I give my sisterly love. You are an inspiring and creative group of women: Liz Allbright, Krissy Andrastek, Ann Archibald, Jenny Archibald, Lora Bruce, Bridget Bullio, Katy Conners, Shelly Conrad, Jen Deslongchamps, Missy Dieterich, Tracy Eckardt, Maria Feeney, Jennifer Elizabeth Foyer, Jamie Gries, Beth Grusenski, Jennifer Hawkins, Alexandra Kammenzind, Regina Karwoski, Kirsten Kohn,

Alexis Kutarna, Heidi Lasnoski, Melissa Magliocco, Carrie Mazza, Lisa O'Keefe, Sue Olbrantz, Michele Pittman, Ann Rauh, Sara-Rae Remmel, Ellen Schlosser, Jeana Skomal, Jenny Thill, and Susan Urbaniak.

It's hard to believe that our modest Milwaukee Aposleship of Prayer (AoP) office serves the entire United States. Past and present members of Team AoP, your gifts are abundant. Many thanks to Melissa Burczyk; Michael Burczyk; Connie Gee; Fr. Phil Hurley, S.J.; Elysse Krueger; Fr. Jim Kubicki, S.J.; Dr. Doug Leonard; Santiago Rodriguez; and Eloise Williamson.

Godchildren, you're next: Monica, Elizabeth, Rhi, Ellen, Ellie, CJ, Liam, Evie, and Cait; thank you for letting me pray with you every day.

How many Mazzas does it take to fill my heart with love and admiration? This many: Mom and Dad; Michael and Carrie, Monica, Maria, Joe, Elizabeth, Thomas, Margaret, Patrick, and Andrew; Matt and Jen, Allie, Nick, Caroline, Charlie, and Cait; Dave and Amy, Nate, Ellie, and Gabe; Joe and Abby; John and Natasha, Liam, and Emmet; Mark and Bee. Add Charlotte Wharton, a wonderful mother-in-law and honorary Mazza, and we've got quite a party.

Thank you, Jesuit world, for teaching me to pray. Thanks especially to Fr. Joe Mueller, S.J., for the annotation and everything else. To the late, great Fr. Will Prospero, S.J., who introduced our family to the Apostleship of Prayer: we miss you. Save a pew for us.

Finally, David, my husband, thank you for wooing me and embarking on this Urbanski mission together. Twenty years into the project, we're still discovering new ways to reflect God's love. Here are my five favorite ways: Clare Macrina Ignatius, Paul Anthony Lawrence, Ann Mary, John Charles, and Rose Alice. Sacred Heart of Jesus, have mercy on us!

A Treasury of Memorized Prayers

Act of Contrition

My God, I am sorry for my sins with all my heart.
In choosing to do wrong and failing to do good,
I have sinned against you whom I should love above all
　　things.
I firmly intend, with your help,
to do penance,
to sin no more,
and to avoid whatever leads me to sin.
Our Savior Jesus Christ suffered and died for us.
In his name, my God, have mercy. Amen.

Glory Be

Glory be to the Father
and to the Son
and to the Holy Spirit:
as it was in the beginning,
is now,
and ever shall be, world without end. Amen.

Grace before Meals

Bless us, O Lord, and these your gifts,
which we are about to receive from your bounty,
through Christ our Lord. Amen.

Grace after Meals

We give you thanks for all your benefits,
Almighty God, who live and reign for ever.
And may the souls of the faithful departed,
through the mercy of God, rest in peace. Amen.

Guardian Angel Prayer

Angel of God,
my guardian dear,
to whom God's love commits me here,
ever this day
be at my side
to light and guard,
to rule and guide. Amen.

Hail Mary

Hail Mary, full of grace,
the Lord is with you.
Blessed are you among women,
and blessed is the fruit of your womb, Jesus.
Holy Mary, Mother of God,
pray for us sinners
now and at the hour of our death. Amen.

Jesus Prayer

Lord Jesus Christ, Son of God, have mercy on me, a
sinner. Amen.

Morning Offering

God, our Father, I offer you my day.
I offer you my prayers, thoughts, words, actions, joys,
    and sufferings
in union with the Heart of Jesus,
who continues to offer Himself in the Eucharist for the
    salvation of the world.
May the Holy Spirit, who guided Jesus,
be my guide and my strength today so that I may wit-
    ness to your love.
With Mary, the mother of our Lord and the Church,
I pray for all Apostles of Prayer
and for the prayer intentions proposed by the Holy
    Father this month. Amen.

Morning Offering for Children

For love of me you came to earth;
You gave your life for me.
So every day you give me now
I give back happily.

Take all my laughter, all my tears,
Each thought, each word, each deed,
And let them be my all-day prayer
To help all those in need. Amen.

Night Prayer

Protect us, Lord, as we stay awake;
watch over us as we sleep,
that awake, we may keep watch with Christ,
and asleep, rest in his peace. Amen.

Our Father

Our Father, who art in heaven,
hallowed be thy name;
thy kingdom come, thy will be done
on earth as it is in heaven.
Give us this day our daily bread;
and forgive us our trespasses,
as we forgive those who trespass against us;
and lead us not into temptation,
but deliver us from evil. Amen.

Prayer to St. Michael, the Archangel

St. Michael the Archangel,
defend us in battle.
Be our defense against the wickedness and snares of the
Devil.
May God rebuke him, we humbly pray,

and do thou,
O Prince of the heavenly hosts,
by the power of God,
thrust into hell Satan,
and all the evil spirits,
who prowl about the world
seeking the ruin of souls. Amen.

Sign of the Cross

In the name of the Father
and of the Son
and of the Holy Spirit. Amen.

Suscipe

Take, Lord, receive all my liberty,
my memory, my understanding, my entire will,
all I have and possess.
You have given all to me.
To you, Lord, I return it.
Everything is yours;
dispose of it according to your will.
Give me only your love and your grace;
that is enough for me. Amen.

$\mathcal{N}$otes

1. PRAYING SPONTANEOUSLY

1. Romano Guardini, *The Art of Praying: The Principles and Methods of Christian Prayer* (Manchester, NH: Sophia Institute, 1994), 98.

2. Adolfo Nicolàs, S.J., "Father General on St. Peter Faber," *America*, December 19, 2013, http://americamagazine.org/content/all-things/father-general-st-peter-faber.

3. Francis, *Evangelii Gaudium*, January 31, 2013, http://www.vatican.va/evangelii-gaudium/en/.

2. PRAYING FROM MEMORY

1. Ben Orlin, "When Memorization Gets in the Way of Learning," *The Atlantic*, September 9, 2013, http://www.theatlantic.com/education/archive/2013/09/when-memorization-gets-in-the-way-of-learning/279425/.

2. Guardini, *The Art of Praying*, 30, 106.

3. Rosario Rodriguez, "Forgiveness," *YouTube*, June 26, 2011, https://www.youtube.com/watch?v=G9WEXW_Uxlg.

4. Immaculée Ilibagiza and Steve Erwin, *Left to Tell: Discovering God amidst the Rwandan Holocaust* (Carlsbad, CA: Hay House, 2006), 95.

5. Mary Kathleen Glavich, S.N.D., *Enriching Faith: Lessons and Activities on the Bible* (Mystic, CT: Twenty-Third Publications, 2014).

6. Anthony T. Kronman, *Education's End: Why Our Colleges and Universities Have Given Up on the Meaning of Life* (New Haven, CT: Yale University Press, 2007), 49–50.

3. PRAYING WITH SCRIPTURE

1. Benedict XVI, *Verbum Domini*, http://w2.vatican.va/content/benedict-xvi/en/apost_exhortations/documents/hf_ben-xvi_exh_20100930_verbum-domini.html.
2. John Paul II, *Vita Consecrata*, http://w2.vatican.va/content/john-paul-ii/en/apost_exhortations/documents/hf_jp-ii_exh_25031996_vita-consecrata.html.

4. PRAYING WITH SONG

1. Norman M. Weinberger, "The Music in Our Minds," *Educational Leadership* 73 (November 1998): 36–40.
2. Jeanette Bicknell, *Why Music Moves Us* (Basingstoke, England: Palgrave Macmillan, 2009), 1.
3. Daniel J. Levitin, *The World in Six Songs: How the Musical Brain Created Human Nature* (New York: Dutton, 2008), 198.
4. Gerard Manley Hopkins, S.J., "Pied Beauty," http://www.poetryfoundation.org/poem/173664.
5. Bridget Smith, A.S.C.J., "Singing in the Classroom," e-mail interview, January 29, 2014.

5. PRAYING WITH SILENCE

1. Paul Wagner, "Elijah (Mendelssohn)," *Music with Ease*, http://www.musicwithease.com/mendelssohn-elijah.html.
2. Mother Teresa of Calcutta, *Life in the Spirit: Reflections, Meditations, Prayers,* ed. Kathryn Spink (San Francisco, CA: Harper and Row, 1983), 19.
3. Diana Senechal, *Republic of Noise: The Loss of Solitude in Schools and Culture* (Lanham, MD: Rowman & Littlefield Education, 2012), 179.
4. Diana Senechal, interview by Alice Karekezi, "Why Kids Need Solitude," *Salon*, December 28, 2011, http://www.salon.com/2011/12/28/why_kids_need_solitude/.
5. Ibid.
6. Tammy St. John, "Compliments," e-mail interview, October 1, 2014.

6. PRAYING WITH REFLECTION

1. Christopher S. Collins, S.J., *Three Moments of the Day: Praying with the Heart of Jesus* (Notre Dame, IN: Ave Maria Press, 2014), 43.

2. Francis, interview by Antonio Spadaro, S.J., "A Big Heart Open to God," *America*, September 30, 2013, http://americamagazine.org/pope-interview.

3. Robert Barron, "7 Keys to the New Evangelization," (keynote, Los Angeles Religious Education Conference, Los Angeles, CA, March 19, 2014).

4. Collins, *Three Moments of the Day*.

7. PRAYING WITH THE APOSTLESHIP OF PRAYER

1. Francis Xavier Gautrelet, S.J., qtd. in www.apostleshipofprayer.org/history.html.

2. "Daily Offering Prayers," *Apostleship of Prayer*, www.apostleshipof-prayer.org/morningofferingprayers.html.

3. Collins, *Three Moments of the Day*, 123.

4. Apostleship of Prayer, "A Pathway with Jesus in Apostolic Readiness" (The Apostleship of Prayer: Document 1, Rome, December 3, 2014) 28, www.apostleshipofprayer.org/rome/AoPRecreationDocumentWeb.pdf.

5. John Paul II, qtd. in www.apostleshipofprayer.org/history.html.

6. "A Pathway with Jesus in Apostolic Readiness," *Apostleship of Prayer*, www.apostleshipofprayer.org/document1.html.

Grace Mazza Urbanski is director of Children's Ministry for the Apostleship of Prayer in the United States. She is a blogger (*Praying with Grace*) and contributor to CatholicMom.com and its Gospel Reflection Team, Catholic Bloggers Network, Catholic 365, and the Association of Catholic Women Bloggers. She serves as a keynote speaker and workshop designer for marriage preparation and married couple events for the Archdiocese of Milwaukee and frequently speaks to parents, teachers, and children throughout the United States in her role with the Apostleship of Prayer.

Urbanski graduated summa cum laude as an undergraduate and also earned a master's degree from Marquette University, where she was formerly a lecturer in the English department. She is a Phi Beta Kappa and a member of several other honors organizations. Urbanski is also a professional vocalist and voice teacher. She is an active member of her parish, St. Mary's Visitation, where she serves on the pastoral council and is former chairman of the Catholic Formation Committee.

Urbanski and her husband, David, have five children. They live in Milwaukee, Wisconsin.